Cattle-Camp
Collection

Keith Garvey

Cover design by Allan Cornwell and Rosie van der Elst

Titles in the series:

Tall Tales from the Bush Volume 1 ISBN 1 875 169 31 8
Tall Tales from the Bush Volume 2 ISBN 1 875 169 32 6
Tall Tales from the Bush Volume 3 ISBN 1 875 169 33 4
                                ISBN 1 875 169 34 2 (Set)

Printed in Australia by McPherson's Printing Group

Produced for the National Direct Marketing Group by:
Allan Cornwell
25 Churchill Road
Mt. Martha Vic 3934

National Direct Marketing Group:
Books Plus (VIC/SA)
Books First (NSW/QLD)
Premier Books (WA)
Meander Books (TAS)

Contents

Contents

Contents

Contents

Contents

"Charley Wilde" previously published in *Songs of a Shearer*.
"Old Time" previously published in *Night of the Dingo*.

Foreward

In Cattle-camp Collection, Keith Garvey has again presented the realism that he strives for in all his work. As I perused the volume, I lived again the days of my youth spent on the stock-camps. Brought back vividly to my mind were the dusty stock-routes, the panting dogs and sweating horses, and the hard-bitten ringers who are now gone from the outback scene. The flickering camp-fires, the blackened ovens where wild meat roasted, the tales told in the silent night around the dying embers, are all startlingly evident in the verse of this doyen of modern-day outback bards.

Keith Garvey spent much of his life on horseback, and he has written of what he lived and witnessed as a stockman. His verses are garnered from practical experience and a photographic memory. If small exaggerations are present, they are something that all poets are guilty of to some extent.

The pattern and attitude of drovers and stockmen exemplified in Garvey's work did not change much throughout Australia, and as a survivor of those uninhibited old times, I consider myself able to speak of them authoratively.

Keith's verses take me back to my droving trips on stock-routes from the Gulf to Victoria, and his characters are replicas of the saddle-hardened workmates that I knew, and of the boss-drovers, gone now, that employed us. Robie Miller from Burketown, the Booth brothers and Walter Cowan going down the Georgina to Coopers Creek and Quilpie with fats from Tanbar, Peter Dawson and Chilla White from Maranoa. And most of all the New England men. Ned Perkins, Tom Cassidy, Jack George, Ellis Robertson, and Jack Kilner from the Hunter River originally. Also Walter Newby, whose grandsons the Ridley brothers still carry on the trade as stockman to-day.

The hoofbeats die, but the ghosts still ride, parading before me in the mind's eye of memory, brought back by Keith Garvey's strikingly descriptive pen.

Colin Newsome
Glen Innes 1987.

Also by Keith Garvey

The Funny Bugger.
Shout for the Adder.
Slowly Sweats the Gun.
Where the Blacksoil Ends.
Night of the Dingo.
My Uncle Harry.
Uncle Harry Rides Again.
Uncle Harry Returns.
More Tales of Uncle Harry.

Rhymes of a Ratbag.
Ditties of a Deadbeat.
Blacksoil Ballads.
Absolutely Australian Verses.
Songs of a Shearer.
Digger Ditties.
Cattle-Camp Collection.

Dinkum Little Aussies.
Vanishing Australians.
New Tales by Uncle Harry.
The Keith Garvey Omnibus.
The Bunyip Wakes.

Muckadilla

We were travelling east from Mitchell when I met her
   In the dust that swirled behind a thousand head
And I loitered at the pub for worse or better
   For the stock were quiet and grass was lush ahead
In the sparkle of her smile a promise waited
   Though she wore a ring I deemed it safe to stay
For the lonely miles had stirred desire unsated
   Where the muddy Muckadilla wends its way.
Sunny days we loafed and stolen nights we courted
   While my mates caroused beneath an autumn moon
'Til the lead was close to Roma, 'twas reported
   And the tail was headed northward to Injune.

Soon the agent came and gave us all a hearing
   He was rabid when he found us off the job
With features grim his words were not endearing
   "Hit the track right now and muster up the mob".
Saddle up and ride, again the long trip starting
   Farewell for now, but I'll return some day
Swift the final meeting sad and then the parting
   Where the muddy Muckadilla wends it way.
For a week it seemed I lingered in a coma
   Building dreams of further dalliance brash and bold
Then a plant came travelling eastward back to Roma
   And the news the drover brought us knocked me cold.

On his weathered face a frosty smile grew chiller
   And his voice contrived a sadness when he spoke
"Barmaid murdered Sunday night at Muckadilla
   Husband landed home and caught her with a bloke".
Point the saddle-stock where dusty routes are wending
   Grim necessity no longer brooks delay
Vanished dream of love and happiness impending

11

Where the muddy Muckadilla winds its way.
Lucky thing for me I didn't stay there longer
   Knew how wrong it was, but still I didn't heed
Moral ties are strong but natural urge is stronger
   Weak mankind surrenders in the time of need.

The packs are slung and loud the horse-bells clatter
   The ghosts depart, the leaders forge ahead
Gone another page of life; it doesn't matter
   The future calls, the distant past is dead.
Fickle charmer cursed with wanton lust and beauty
   By a stroke of violence swift returned to clay
Paid a price too high for scorning faith and duty
   Where the muddy Muckadilla wends its way.

Ballad of Marsupial Bill

Well boys, I reckon it's my shout
   Come sit down in the shade
I'll tell a tale about a bloke
   Who plied a gory trade.
Marsupial Bill a scalper was
   As all you fellers know
He shot the 'roos and took their pelts;
   Until two years ago.

About that time the drought was bad
   And all the land was dry
The cockies eyes were starin' mad
   As long they watched the sky.
Old Bill in town got full of rum
   And started out at dark
In scrub so thick yer couldn't hear
   A pack of dingoes bark
To seek his camp, but lost he got
   And couldn't find the way
And off his head he was with thirst
   Before the break of day.

Delirious he soon became
   He was a dreadful sight
With in his eyes the buttery tears
   That herald sandy blight.
The hungry meat-ants follered close
   Not wishin' to be late
To cop a major share of Bill
   When he lost his bout with fate.

Above him in the scorchin' sky
   The bush crows dived and swerved
All waitin' for a juicy meal

That shortly would be served
And out of every holler spout
Big black goannas came
Anticipatin' tasty steaks
From Bill's exhausted frame.

His tongue was swelled, his legs were weak
He couldn't hold a trick
And he reckoned shortly that he would
Be boardin' with Old Nick.
When up ahead beneath a tree
An old man 'roo he saw
It studied him with solemn eyes
Then beckoned with it's paw.
And as old Bill was strugglin' hard
His senses to maintain
It hopped away a dozen yards
And beckoned once again.

So through the bush behind the 'roo
Old Bill went staggerin' hard
And wonderin' why this animal
Would show such kind regard
To someone who had shot its mates
In dozens every week
But that old 'roo had Christian ways
And it turned the other cheek

It led the hunter to his camp
And he remembers still
How the 'roo took down the water-bag
And handed it to Bill.
The old boy guzzled long and loud
And slobbered in his beard
But found when he had quenched his thirst
The 'roo had disappeared.
Next week the hunter sold his gun
And threw his knife away

14

And now he is a member of
  The R.S.P.C.A.

So all you shooters heed this tale
  For when yer on the booze
Yer likely to see stranger things
  Than Christian kangaroos.

NEIL PERCIVAL

The Burial of Greenhide McGee

Far to the north when at break of day the skies to the
    east are red
And in vagrant breezes the brigalows sway at
    evening when day is dead
That's where the scrubber-runners rode, to their
    calling duty bound.
Reckless resistance to fate their code, courage stout
    to astound.

Ever the bravest hearts of all, soldiers who won no
    fame
Men of the spurs and greenhide fall, playing a
    hazardous game
And the mightiest stockman their ranks could boast
    in that land unfettered and free
Wilder than many, braver than most was Greenhide
    Jack McGee.

Now Greenhide Jack was lover bold, as the ladies
    regretfully knew
And when passion subsided he left them cold, a
    scoundrel with heart untrue.
'Til at length in the bar of the Ringer's Rest, as he
    drank with his mates one day
He met with a barmaid from farther west, and she
    yarded his heart for aye.

Blackall Bonnie was full of quile, dark and slender
    and neat
And when Greenhide Jack flashed a winning smile
    it knocked her clean off her feet.

So on moonlit musters with stars above he rode
without doubt or fear
Then off to the shanty to plead his love with a
worshipping heart held dear.

'Til her virtue was sundered to sate his lust on a
night when the stars were wan
'Tis a story of faith and foolish trust that was old
when the world began.
"Tomorrow," he said, "to town I'll make, and a
date arrange with the priest
And I'll knock down a mickey to cut the steak for
the boys at the weddin' feast.

"There's a fortnight left in the job at hand, and a
weighty cheque to draw
Then united for life in the church we'll stand, and
I'll scatter the brush no more.
"I haven't the time to repent and rue in a wild life
lived too fast"
"It's a dream", said Bonnie, "a dream come true,
so speak no word of the past".

"Look to the future, the past is dead, and our lives
will be long and free"....
But the hand of the Reaper with talons spread was
reaching out for McGee.
Bright was the night of his wedding eve, on the
moonlighters' lonely camp
Where the branches a shadowy pattern weave on the
Mitchell grasses damp.

He tightened the girth with a smile and said, "To-
night is the final ride
I'll stand a mickey right on his head, and termorrer
I'll claim me bride".

The scrubbers were spied on a grassy swale with the
    timber far to the rear
And they heard the stockmen and fled like quail as
    the sound of hooves grew near.

Stockwhips sounded a rat-a-tat-tat in the moonlight
    dappled by dust
And hard on the wing was a mickey fat that ran with
    its tail upthrust.
"He's mine for the banquet", shouted McGee,
    "Just watch me skittle him now,"
And he took no heed of the bloodwood tree with the
    jagged low-hanging bough.

And the spike of timber that ran him through was
    sharp as a bayonet blade
And Blackall Bonnie whose heart was true was by
    fate in her love betrayed.
Destined to follow a lonely path, a mother but never
    a bride
For the gods of chance and a mickey calf had ended
    her lover's last ride.

His cobbers gathered at break of dawn where a
    shallow grave was struck
Then spoke the boss looking sad and forlorn, "we
    ain't got a coffin, worse luck".
Then spoke an old ringer, a hard man was he, and
    sadly addicted to beer
Said, "always we knew him as Greenhide McGee,
    and it gives me a real bright idea.

"There's the skin of a bullock we slaughtered for
    meat, and to do a good ringer right proud
We should send him to hell lookin' sprightly and
    neat wrapped up in a nice greenhide shroud.

18

Not a dignified casket, it's sad to relate, but it gives
    him a semblance of style
A very tough suit for a very tough mate, it should
    keep out the worms for a while.''

So rolled in the greenhide they buried him there,
    rugged men with a grim rugged code
A thought for the woman, a short mumbled
    prayer....''Saddle up boys again, hit the road''.

The long years have vanished, and times now are
    changed; no more do the wild cattle run
On the vast scrubby land where the brush-bashers
    ranged grows the wheat rippling gold in the sun.
And relentless the ploughs and the tractors dig deep
    where the old shanty bar used to be
And their bellowing thunder will not wreck the sleep
    of the ringer called Greenhide McGee.

Ballad of the Desert Lair

(Or Fate of an Old Time Shearer)

"I've carried me gear", said the Desert Lair
    "On every outback way
On deserts dry under furnace sky
    Where famine and thirst hold sway
Pastures poor where camel manure
    Is the fuel for to boil yer tea
And devils command in a lonely land
    Where no white man ought to be.
Over and back on the Birdsville track
    Where many a traveller died
By western town when the floods were down
    And the river was ten miles wide.
In search of work no tramp I'll shirk
    Be it watercourse, ridge or plain
I've travelled the long leads west of Bourke
    and I'll travel 'em back again.
    I'll travel 'em back again".

Montreal May he met one day
    From Canada's snows she came
She fell for the flair of the Desert Lair
    A young and romantic dame.
Seeking new life in a land of strife
    Far from the Northland cold
Where the huskies wail on the Yukon trail
    In the search for the Klondyke gold.
"I'll sally forth to the sheds up north"
    Said the lair," just one trip more
"I'll win us a cheque or bust me neck
    On the greasy shearin' floor.
"I'll take me chance where the heat-waves dance

20

And yer never see dew or rain
I've travelled the long leads west of Bourke
　　And I'll travel 'em back again.
　　I'll travel 'em back again".

Said the girl, "beware, for this land I fear
　　Where the drought devils dance at noon
There are dead mens' bones on desert stones
　　And by many a dry lagoon.
Too late it will be to think of me
　　When you lie on a nameless track
While the circle of crows in number grows
　　And your tongue is swollen and black.
And a sun-rotted swag and water-bag
　　Shall the place of your resting mark
Where the lizard and snake will a bounty take
　　While the dingo feasts in the dark".
But the Lair said, "fear not the desert drear
　　Where the careless expire in pain
I've travelled the long leads west to Bourke
　　And I'll travel 'em back again.
　　I'll travel 'em back again".

She watched him go in the sunset glow
　　Under a reeling sky
Where gibbers grey seemed like beasts of prey
　　And Time held the hour-glass high.
For the desert hard offers no regard
　　For pitifully weak mankind
Down that western track he never came back
　　To the girl that he left behind
Gone to his rest on a sandhill's crest
　　In a country still unsurveyed
Sun-whitened swag and water bag
　　By the bleaching skeleton laid.
But old sinners say that at close of day
　　His ghost sings a wild refrain
"I've travelled the long leads west of Bourke
　　And I'll travel 'em back again.

21

"I've carried a swag and tucker-bag
 On every outback way
On deserts dry under furnace sky
 From dawn 'til the death of day.
In search of work no road I'll shirk
 Be it mountain or scrub or plain
I've travelled the long leads west of Bourke
 And I'll travel 'em back again.
I'll travel 'em back again."

NEIL PERCIVAL

Ballad of the Bagman's Watch

Beside his swag the old man lay
   beneath a shady gum
His dirty hair was lank and grey
   his breath befouled with rum.
His gummy optics seemed to gloat
   bespeaking thirst unslaked
And in the creases of his throat
   the grime of years was caked.

He asked me if the time I knew
   and when I shook my head
In deep disgust he waved a hand
   like the claw of something dead.
He chewed a gum-leaf, spat it out
   and sadly wagged his tongue
"I always had a timepiece, mate
   in days when I wuz young.

"I useter have a big gold watch
   a presentation job
The chain wuz nearly two feet long
   with emeralds on the fob.
I staggered orf from Shanley's pub
   one day, and fell asleep
Close by there wuz a wombat's den
   with tunnels dark and deep.

"Me dreams were of a luscious girl
   a sheila of great note
When suddenly a stealthy hand
   I feels inside me coat
And I reckoned that it was this girl
   caressin' me with love

23

Then I awakes to warnin' croaks
   made be the crows above.

"Believe me mate, I sprung up quick
   and thought I wuz insane
An old buck wombat's standin' near
   and he's got me watch and chain.
"His eyes were winkin' bright with greed
   and he scratched his hairy lug
Yer could fairly read the bludger's thoughts
   "I've found a first-class mug".

"A grisly grin wuz on his dial
   as the plunder he surveyed
Just like a master criminal
   when a haul of cash is made.
I made a rush to tackle him
   just as he turned to flee
But I miscued and banged me head
   against a leanin' tree.

" 'Twas after dark when I come round
   me skull was filled with pain
Gone was me dream of faithful love
   and gone me watch and chain.
But oft in later years I heard
   of a wombat fellers saw
With a golden chain around its neck
   and a watch held in its paw.

"But one thing I assure yer, mate
   now that me tale is told
Wombats, like sheilas, seem to have
   an eye for gain and gold
So steer clear of drink, don't dream of love
   for me story makes it plain
Yer can lose yer soul and heart and head
   and yer bloody watch and chain."

24

NEIL PERCIVAL

Outback
Doctor

I'll simply call him Doctor Jack,
   in case there's a relation...
A medico who came outback
   in search of reformation.
Before the motor-car arrived
   and doctors found no answer
To many cruel complaints that thrived,
   Consumption, flu and cancer.

A doubtful past our hero knew,
   deep-thinking people noted.
Perhaps a lady-love untrue
   his fall from grace promoted
Perhaps in youth a reckless rake
   by faithless friends exploited
Perhaps he buried a mistake
   that on his conscience loitered.

Despite his alcoholic curse
   a scholar and a gentleman
And even when for drink the worse
   a greatly sentimental man.
And ceaselessly his work upheld
   the cause of sick humanity
His moral weakness never quelled
   his sense of Christianity.

On pitted tracks in bushland wide
   by winding creek and river
He oft made long a weary ride
   a baby to deliver.
He calmly patched up injured men
   Where flood or fire or gale went

26

And filled the kids with jalap when
   they had a stomach ailment.

And be it lady grand or whore,
   the women he attended
A smiling psychologic cure
   imagined sickness mended.
On winter nights when hell would freeze
   he many lonely trips had
To aid the shearers in D.Ts.
   And ringers dosed with clap bad.

To treat a patient never loth,
   he seldom slept or rested
And like his Hippocratic oath,
   his horse was sorely tested
He hit the liquor hard himself
   to break the bleak monotony
His efforts garnered little pelf
   because his patients hadn't got any.

He went at last to time's dim mists,
   too long a sad self-giver
Of medication that assists
   cihrossis of the liver.
Winning no fortune, fame or praise,
   no headlines in the paper.
His bloodwood marker long decays
   where possums curse and caper.

Perchance in Heaven's cloudless blue
   he holds a drinking session,
Despite his sins a credit to
   the medical profession.
Perhaps at night his ghost appears
   at lonely camp and station
Another of the pioneers
   who helped to make our nation.

NEIL PERCIVAL

Lofty Lloyd
(Ballad of an old shearing mate)

Like a ghost from the past you have sought me at last
  And believe me I'm happy to know
You recall days of yore when together we shore
  In the sheds on the Bland long ago.
  In the sheds on the Bland long ago.
With your letter I'm quite overjoyed, Lofty Lloyd
  For oft I have pondered your fate
And I feared a true friendship destroyed, Lofty Lloyd
  By our last heated Union debate.
  By our last headed Union debate.

All the old guns are gone, just a few carry on
  at the trade that is secondary now
Foreign combines hold sway, growing stronger each day
  And the wool to the cotton must bow.
  The wool to the cotton must bow.
Oh, remember the lurks we employed, Lofty Lloyd
  To establish survival each day
As with hopes of a start null and void, Lofty Lloyd
  We swagged it from Cobar to Hay.
  We swagged it from Cobar to Hay.

How when sick from the booze we shore hard wrinkled ewes
  And big rams that defied all our blows
And we bitterly swore we would tiger no more
  On the studs where the Castlereagh flows
  On the studs where the Castlereagh flows.
Think again how our spirits were bouyed, Lofty Lloyd
  When at Christmas we loafed for a spell
Wearing elegant garments uncloyed, Lofty Lloyd
  By the wool and its raw pungent smell.
  By the wool and its raw pungent smell.

The races up north when we boldly set forth
   To send broke all the books on the line
And the marathon spree that we held out at Bree
   On strong home-brew and second grade wine
   On strong home-brew and second grade wine.
Oh, remember the beer we enjoyed, Lofty Lloyd
In the south when the sheds were cut out
And the hard times we stood unemployed, Lofty Lloyd
   When the country was gripped by the drought
   When the country was gripped by the drought.

Remember the pain and the backache and strain
   The stale curry and rice every night
And the little bush flies that bombarded our eyes
   On the plains when we caught sandy blight,
   On the plains when we caught sandy blight.
With the thought of a comeback I've toyed, Lofty Lloyd
   But the strength from my arm now has fled
So let's drink to a future destroyed, Lofty Lloyd
   For the days of the shearing are dead.
   The days of the shearing are dead, Lofty Lloyd
   The days of the shearing are dead.

NEIL PERCIVAL

31

The Pommy Cook

The boss-of-the-board was tall and broad
  and the shearers feared him with one accord
    While the loppies shivered and shook
He belted the Cunnamulla Skite
  and 'Snowy' Black and 'Darkie' White
    But he reckoned without the cook, boys
    He reckoned without the cook.

Limehouse Jim was slender and slim
  born in the slums of London grim
    Placid and pensive look
Worked his passage to Aussie clime
  in a steamer's galley befouled with grime
    That's where he learned to cook, boys
    That's where he learned to cook.

Can't think now what started the row.
  boss called Jimmy a Pommy cow
    And a bloody immigrant sook
Little bloke doffed his apron and cap
  "Outside chum, if yer want a scrap"
    Confident bloke the cook, boys
    Confident bloke the cook.

Strike me roan, but I have to own
  when the boss stripped down all muscle and bone
    The future was lookin' crook
But under the slush-lamps glitterin' bright
  we saw that night a bloke could fight
    Never misjudge the cook, boys
    Never misjudge the cook.

Wind arose from the boss's blows
  as Jimmy's straight left tattooed his nose
    And swift was the cook's right hook

Just the same the bully was game
  But he lost his claim to fistic fame
    For he reckoned without the cook, boys
  He reckoned without the cook.

The blacksoil plain was turned to mud
  By snot and blood that flew like a flood
    From punches the big bloke took
After the seventeenth knock-down
  he lay a battered and beaten clown
    Easy meat for the cook, boys
  Easy meat for the cook.

Then the Pommy child shook hands and smiled
  sayin' "Chum, I sparred with Jimmy Wilde
    And Driscoll read me the book".
So men who shear from far and near
  Be sure, sore ribs are hard to bear
    So always respect the cook, boys
  Always respect the cook.

Final Delivery
(A Ringer's Prayer)

Over the lignum stars are bright
And the camp-fire's glitter pierces the night
  In the gums by the slope of the river
Plaintive the watchman's popular tune
Softy sung neath a vanishing moon
Trouble and trial will be over soon
  For to-morrow's the day we deliver.

Big gaunt steers from the Queensland side
Many a night they made us ride
  When months ago we started
Water was bad and feed was short
And our effort was daily in hardship wrought
But uncomplaining the battle we fought
  Like early Christrians martyred.

Under the dust-cloud rolling dun
Tireless they walked beneath cloud and sun
  Where the soul of the saint would wither
Now they docile camp on the sandhill's crown
Footsore and tired from the long trip down
On wearying leagues of stock-route brown
  And to-morrow's the day we deliver.

Danger and poverty, hardship and strife
All are part of a ringer's life
  Small is the gain collected
Of honour and chivalry little we know
Moneygrub's puppets unsung we go
Drunken and banal, immoral and low
  By society's hand rejected.

But when for the final trip we arrive
Hopeful I am that our souls will survive

The test of God, the life-giver
Perhaps our labours will pay the account
As the Golden Stair our worn boots mount
To the yard where St. Peter checks the count
When at last comes the day we deliver.

NEIL PERCIVAL

O'Leary

(A famous Queensland stockman)

O'Leary died on a stormy night
When the vagabond moon was out of sight
  In a blinding torrent's swell
Caught in a rush where wet hooves splashed
And wild eyes gleamed and long horns clashed
  O'Leary's stock-horse fell.
Trampled to death on the slippery clay
Battered and broken and crushed he lay
  In the stampede's churning wake
Swift was his passing, lone is his grave
On the ironstone ridge where the bloodwoods wave
  And the fronds of the wilgas shake.
Never a fellow to cry enough
Horses and women he 'liked 'em rough'
  Proud with a horseman's pride
'Tis reckoned the angels swooned with fright
And the devil himself turned pasty white
  When Jack O'Leary died.

Old bush ways with the years have fled
On bluegrass leagues where the wild mobs fed
  The big machines are parked
Only a few old hands recall
The time of O'Leary's fatal fall
  And his shallow grave unmarked.
But legend has it, and legend tells
That on violent nights when storm-wind swells
  And swift is the driving rain
For treacherous ground showing no regard
On a phantom stock-horse galloping hard
  O'Leary rides again.
Spectral hooves that scatter the slush
Making no sound in the bushland's hush
  Silent on acres vast
Shadowy rider crouching low

On shadowy steed, to the mists they go
  Of Australia's vanished past.

NEIL PERCIVAL

Old Man Saltbush

Old Man Saltbush grim and grey
   True Australian native
Mournful in the waking day
   Quite undecorative
To the sun's hot rays immune
   Little moisture needing
Spectral 'neath the summer moon
   When the stock are feeding.

Long ago you saw the teams
   And the early settlers
Where your saline foliage gleams
   Toiled the railroad fettlers
When the drovers camp-fires blazed
   In the early morning
On your leaves the lean steers grazed
   Phantoms of the dawning.

On the blacksoil rooted deep
   Rugged growth attaining,
In the hungry travelling sheep
   Feeble life sustaining
Gaunt beasts from the camel-train
   Swift your juices nourished
In a land of little rain
   Bold and bright you flourished.

Should the drought king hold command
   Or the skies be leaden
Old man saltbush strong will stand
   Until Armageddon.

The Farmer's Dream

(A fantasy of drought)

The farmer wished that the rain might fall
  To bring peace and plenty to hill and plain
And sad were the bushland creatures small
  As freedom they sought from the drought-king's chain.
So the farmer dreamed that the drought had broke
  As he lay enjoying a welcome nap
The bullfrogs' throats went crackety-croak
  And the wood-ducks' wings went quackety-flap.

The water flooded the swamps and lakes
  And the bagmen unbagged their bottles of rum
The black-duck happy played ducks and drakes
  And the numbat battered opponents numb.
The carpet snake gave a spissity-hiss
  As he polished his scales with the housemaid's mop
The love-birds all played kissety-kiss
  And the big grey 'roo danced hippety-hop.

The rain-god had granted the farmer's wish
  And the pelican said, "It's wet, by gosh"
The old black shag went splashetty-splish
  And the bunyip in the mud went splosh.
The tiger-cat's walk was a prancing prowl
  And the death-adder's song was a syrupy croon
The dingo's growl was a happiness howl
  At the comforting clouds that covered the moon.

The magpie applauded the rising flood
  And the old black crow went squacketty-squark
The mopoke claimed he had royal blood
  As he bashed the lug of the jabiru stork.
The cattle and sheep all happily cheered

39

As they ate the succulent grasses sweet
And the billy-goat oiled and trimmed his beard
And his beautiful nanny went forth to meet.

There were new gum-sprouts for the native bears
And every creature was happy again
So the wallaby called for three long cheers
For the storm-god's bounty of wonderful rain.
Then the farmer woke and his eyes grew sad
As he gazed down the barren drought-seared slope
It was only a fanciful dream he had
Promoted by desperate and wishful hope.

Ring 'em in the Gidgee

(Told to the author by a hard-riding and amorous Queensland ringer.)

Rain has brought a season lush
    River's flowin' wide
Time to run the scrubbers, boys
    Saddle up and ride.
Grab the fastest horse yer got
    Drop all fear and doubt
Ring 'em in the gidgee
    'Til their tongues hang out.

Leery cows with mickey calves
    Bullocks fat and fine
Lurkin' in the thickets dark
    North of Condamine.
Knowin' every rat-hole
    Where it's safe to hide
Plantin' in the deepest bush
    When the musterers ride.

Sneakin' out at night to feed
    Underneath the stars
Fearin' close confinement
    In the brigalow bars
Let the heelers off the chains
    Tighten up the girth
Then ring 'em in the gidgee
    For all yer bloody worth.

Try to grab 'em by the tail
    Chase 'em through the brush
Wheel 'em when they break away
    Block 'em when they rush.

Old and evil mallet stags
  Big bulls wild and hard
Ring 'em in the gidgee
  Head 'em for the yard.

Hit the town on Saturday
  A dance is swingin' fine
Lots of sheilas round the hall
  Who like a drop of wine.
Dainty little heifers
  Shy, demure and sweet
Tough old cows who've run to beef
  Wide across the seat.

Coax 'em to a moonlit spot
  Promise 'em a shout
The ring 'em in the gidgee
  'Til their tongues hang out.
Try to grab 'em by the tail
  Chase 'em through the brush
Wheel 'em when they break away
  Block 'em when they rush.

Ring 'em in the gidgee
  Love's a lusty steal
Ring 'em in the gidgee
  'Til they start to squeal.
Seek no gaudy double bed
  What's wrong with mother earth?
Ring 'em in the gidgee
  For all yer bloody worth....
"Yaa..hoo!! Ring 'em in the gidgee
  For all yer bloody worth!!".

An Old Pair of Spurs

(I still retain the first pair of "Darbies" I owned, bought half a century ago...Author's note)

Sold for a song to a second-hand store
   By one of a careless band
Leathery ringer long gone before
Who rode in the days when the land was raw
   And hope was an empty hand.
Perished the straps and buckles bent
   Broken the rowels and worn
Travelling the tracks where drovers went
Oft in the past to old mates lent
   Rusted now and forlorn.

Spattered with blood on stock-routes brown
   When breakaways made their try
Smeared with mud when floods were down
And the cattle were pushed to the sand-hill's crown
   Under a threatening sky.
Left one night in a harlot's room
   By a ringer whose cheque was "blued"
As he fled ere the daylight pierced the gloom
   When lust and longing ceased to bloom
   After a short interlude.

Oft in the ribs of a rough one thrust
   While the boys on the rails cheered loud
Round a stockyard hazy with rising dust
"Stay with the bastard!! Ride him or bust!!"
   Fun for a motley crowd.
Reflecting the light in an outback bar

43

From the kerosene lamps above
Where the barmaid's smile was a dazzling star
Hiding a mind too shrewd by far
    For acceptance of doubtful love.

Gallant old goosenecks; now you hang
    Over my desk as I write
And I think of a time when the box-trees rang
To the boisterous yells of a youthful gang
    Gone forever from sight.
Gone forever from dale and hill
    Camp and river and plain
Old and crippled I linger still
But while ever I live old memories will
    Like the worn-out spurs remain.

NEIL PERCIVAL

The Synthetic Shearer

To the bright city lights came the Burrangong Lair
   From a shed on the wild Weddin range
And he pitched for a sheila with carroty hair
   In the bar of the Royal Exchange.
He boasted of tallies he shore in the West
   And the sheds that he rung far and near
But Ginger the barmaid was hardly impressed
   And with boredom she served him the beer.

Tall tales he related of studs out from Bree
   With their rough rams and hard wrinkled ewes
Where he chalked up two-fifty for all hands to see
   After spending a night on the booze.
He told how he deuced 'em at tough Bungendore
   At Goonal it was sixty a run
In the lambs on the Bogong three hundred he shore
   And at Midkin he led every gun.

To the whiskey he switched, with a chase of stout
   As he polished each wether's rough neck
And drunker he grew as each shed was cut out
   And to mammoth proportions his cheque.
But the drink was his downfall, I have to confess
   Though with each glass more hoggets he shore
Soon with bottle and boggi his efforts grew less
   And he slumped in a daze on the floor.

"A bright boy", said Ginger, "the world's full of fools
   As the girls in the bar all can tell
"It's time, Jackie Howe, that you hung up the tools
   And retired to the hut for a spell.

But this small cozy bar must be kept clean and neat
  If at last you have done slinging bull
My unbeatable shearer, climb on to your feet
  You can start sweeping up all the wool".

NEIL PERCIVAL

The Woolpresser's Tale

Once when at Berrigal Creek I was pressin'
   I saw a strange happenin', I don't mind confessin'.
Billy the Rat performed dreadful contortions
   Pursued be a fantod of monstrous proportions.
For more than a fortnight bad grog he was drinkin'
   And into a coma was rapidly sinkin'.
With hot castor-oil and black coffee we filled him
   A big overdose you'd have swore would have killed him.
Hot mutton broth be the gallon we fed him
   And like an old horse with a sharp knife we bled him.
He gurgled and choked 'til we reckoned he'd smother
   Then after a week he began to recover.
I asked "Where's the fantod yer swore kept appearin'
   The big one that over yer shoulder was leerin'."
Said Bill "In me beard he kept gettin' entangled
   So I hung to his throat 'til the bludger was strangled.
"And that was what caused me recovery, I'd say
   For that fantod ain't here to annoy me to-day".

Charley Wilde

(A Legendary horse-breaker in the Moree
district)

Weathered the walls 'neath timeless skies
    Under the box-tree's bough
Sagging the bench where the bridle lies
    Long discarded now.
Rotting the stockyard rail and post
    Battered by sun and rain
But when darkness falls perchance the ghost
    Of the Master rides again.

Long and lean with wispy moustache
    And a horseman's stilted walk
Never flamboyant loud or flash
    Seldom a man to talk.
No gaudy showring stylist fine
    Always reserved and mild
Partial at times to beer and wine
    That was Charley Wilde.

Learned his trade on the Nor'-west plains
    Where the Mehi pursues its course
Born with the feel of bridle-reins
    And the bushman's love for a horse.
Riders there were of loftier sway
    But never a one more bold
And Charley Wilde got on to stay
    While ever the gear would hold.
Confident style and rigid seat
    Courage that stout prevailed
Countless bad ones broke and beat
    Where others had tried and failed
Buckers and bolters small chance had
    Quiet ones care beguiled

Brutal on horses spoiled or bad
   That was Charley Wilde.

Rolling eyes and tossing manes
   Shoulders awash with sweat
Labour of love a pittance gains
   No time for vain regret.
Plying no raffle of fancy gear
   As the rough ones twisted high
No audience standing by to cheer
   Under the dusty sky.
Kooroogamma, Keytah, Goonal
   Anywhere bloods were bred
Scorning the risk of a stunning fall
   Or the pain of a broken head
Stoic until the fight was won
   Or when fortune no longer smiled
Proud of a patient job well done
   That was Charley Wilde.

Age and injury take their toll
   The best must with time abide
Headstall and halter and roping pole
   Are laid with the years aside.
Hang up the saddle with heavy heart
   And spurs that flashed in the sun
The horseback men from the scene depart
   For ever their long day done.
Reckless of danger to life and limb
   No fortune vast they made
Deep in the mists of memory dim
   The muffled hoofbeats fade.
Only the legends now remain
   by the old hands long compiled
'Til the day that the dead men ride again
   Farewell, Charley Wilde.

The Boundary Rider's Horse

The boundary rider's horse
Is no thoroughbred of course
    Just a hack
He's mostly lean and poor
And often has a sore
    On his back.
Quite patiently he plods
While his rider nods
    Half asleep
He doesn't boldy neigh
But slowly makes his way
    Round the sheep.

He hears no trumpet played
And leads no grand parade
    At the show
You will notice at a glance
That he doesn't proudly prance
    Or snort and blow.
He's used to slender meals
And suffers greasy heels
    A cruel complaint
No bards his praises sing
A steed fit for a king
    Is what he ain't.

Though no awards he wins
Despite his sins
    He does his bit
And in the pastoral game
Although he earns no fame
    He's full of grit.
And when (it's sadly true)

He can no longer do
　　His jobs assorted
No mourners to attend
He meets a sticky end
　　For pet food slaughtered.

NEIL PERCIVAL

Hardships
(Or the Old Overlanders)

At a picture I gaze in an old book to-night
  Of a wide stretch of blacksoil with rain streaming white
On a slow plodding pack-plant strung out in the mud
  Splashing wet in wild waters that promise a flood.
And the drovers humped up in the cold driving sleet
  On bone-weary horses dog-poor and dead beat.
Floundering deep in discomfort, privation and pain
  Facing long weary weeks ere they reached home again
Oh, people in cities and towns never knew
  Of the hardships the old overlanders went through.

From the Gulf of the Murray the old stock-routes ran
  And the trips in those days were the test of a man
When hard was the damper and muddy the stream
  And quick medical aid at its best was a dream
And twelve hours in the saddle was quite a short spell
  With the corn-meat all flyblown and fearful it's smell
And the dysentery promised a miserable plight
  Plus flies black and sticky that spread sandy blight.
  In the bleak Bogong mountains or on the Paroo
  Waited hardships the old overlanders went through.

When the big lanky bullocks broke camp in the night
  As thunder growled deep and the lightning flashed bright
Then a false step meant death as displaying great speed
  The ribby old stock-horse would head for the lead,
Rough terrain that causes the weak heart to quail
  And jagged the brigalow that waits to impale.
And the rider unheeding these traps on the way
  Placed his life as a forfeit at five bob a day
Would the absentee owners have cared had they knew
  The hardships the old overlanders went through.

55

Now the drover to-day is a much softer man
   For in comfort he rides in a big caravan
With the missus to cook, and the kids along too
   And the beer in the fridge is a nice tasty brew.
With a horn on his trail-bike to steady the lead
   A luxurious change from the old days indeed.
With facilities modern he does a good job
   And in excellent condition delivers the mob
He would think himself lucky if only he knew
   Of the hardships the old overlanders went through.

The Drovers' Gift

The barmaid at the Ringers' Rest
   was quite a lah-de-dah
With ample rump, and raucous voice
   just like a pet galah.
She told two passing drover men
   Black Jack and Rusty Ned
"I've made a matrimonial move,
   next week I'm going to wed
A squatter rich named Randolph Knutts.
   from west of Wingadee
He claims he's never met a girl
   as beautiful as me".

"Old Randy Knutts!," said Rusty Ned,
   "A lustful, sexy beast
He's had four wives, three servants
   and six young girls at least".
"Oh yes, I know", the barmaid said
   with worship in her voice
"But his women were unfaithful types,
   this time he's made good choice.
I'm sure that true and faithful
   and devoted he will be
I'm confident beyond all doubt
   he wouldn't cheat on me".

Black Jack winked swift at Rusty Ned,
   Ned's doubtful smile stayed long
While the senseless woman chattered
   loud as any currawong.
"I'm very, very hopeful
   that you drovers good and kind
A wedding present suitable
   for me will surely find.

57

"Some necessary item
  for a happy bride, I'm sure...
Black Jack looked hard at Rusty Ned
  then headed out the door.

To where the horses switched their tails
  beneath a tall belar
He soon returned, and with a grin
  he dropped upon the bar
A shiny set of hobbles
  made to hold the wildest horse
Hand-forged and stoutly tempered
  to resist all kinds of force.
Stong greenhide straps constructed well,
  immune to strife and strain
A double swivel hardly worn
  in heavy links of chain.

"What's that thing for", the barmaid asked
  "what for, upon my soul"...
"They're for a stallion", Jack replied
  "a horse we can't control"...
Tall stood the ringer, lank and lean,
  his weathered face was lined
With shrewd expression that announced
  the wisdom of his kind.
"That there's yer present, miss," he said
  "and there ain't no ifs or buts
Yer goin' to need them hobbles bad
if yer marry Randy Knutts".

58

NEIL PERCIVAL

Ballad of McGinty

McGinty came from county Clare
  To the big plains west of Bourke
Where the red earth writhes in the garish glare
Of withering sunlight hard to wear
  And drought-fiends ferocious lurk.
Brash and young with confidence strong
  To the cattle-camps wild he went
Where the graft was grim and hours were long
But like many another man gone wrong
  In hardship he sought content.

Big-gun ringer he soon became
  Born with a feel for the reins
Always reckless, always game
Unknown his past, assumed his name
  A man of the Western plains.
But a burdening conscience weighted his mind
  A sad sin gone before
Too late he regretted his deed unkind
To the pregnant girl he had left behind
  On Ireland's turbulent shore.

So he worked for rich men by money spoiled
  Who showed no love or regard
For underpaid ringers who ceaseless toiled
On stock-routes barren where dust-wrack roiled
  From the Gulf to Wodonga yard.
But at night when horse-bells tinkled clear
  And the stars their glitter displayed
He lay and whispered a silent prayer
For Sally O'Dowd in county Clare
  The lass that his lust betrayed.

All too swiftly the short years flew
    Where life at the best was hard
Dissolute drunken and old he grew
No lasting comfort or love he knew
    In stockcamp and dusty yard.
Then there came one day an Irish lad
    To the rolling plains far flung
And the Gaelic wit and charm he had
Soon were the ringers' hearts made glad
    By the songs that Paddy sung.

McGinty liked his confident grin
    And the way that his work was done
Last to finish, first to begin
On long nightwatches black as sin
    And days of sweat in the sun.
So McGinty asked the boy one day
    As they rested from toil and wear
"What caused ye, Paddy to take and stray
To a foreign country far away
    From the green ould sod so dear?"

"No people I had", the boy replied
    "When me mother passed away
A worthless scoundrel her faith denied
Yet she loved him right 'til the day she died
    Now his debt he never will pay.
"Sister or brother I cannot claim
    I knew not a father's care
Sally O'Dowd was me mother's name
She bore her son in unmarried shame
    And she came from county Clare".

Next day was mustered a paddock vast
    Where the brigalow was dense and green
And conscience cruel on McGinty cast
It's shadow of sin from long years past

61

And he cursed the man he had been.
Out of the thickets the scrubbers dashed
   Where they'd hidden since break of day
Stirrups and spurs in sunlight flashed
Like light artillery stockwhips crashed
   The hunt was under way.

Then a wild bull broke from the nervous herd
   Horns lowered, and with fiery eyes
On sunbaked earth that hot hooves stirred
After the breakaway Paddy spurred
   Riding rash and unwise.
Down went his mount in the swirling dust
   And the fall was stunning and hard
As the piker charged with murderous lust
But McGinty was riding as ringers must
   When death holds the winning card.

Down went the piker's foam streaked head
   Lowered for the fatal thrust
Fleet as a swallow the stock-horse fled
Sweating sides by spurs made red
   Wild hooves hurling the dust.
Straight for the big horns curving wide
   Went McGinty diving low
And there on the sand the wastrel died
As with desperate courage he vainly tried
   That mountain of beef to throw.

With a fleeting vision of youth gone by
   When without a worry or care
Where the mavis warbled in greenwoods high
He strolled by the bog 'neath a summer sky
   With a colleen from county Clare.
Back to the mob the piker went
   Under the stockmens' whips
And as over the dead man Paddy bent

It seemed that a smile of calm content
  Was etched on the silent lips.

They buried him deep where a krui gleamed
  Green in the sunset gold
And the sturdy myalls sentinels seemed
Watchers over a man redeemed
  Whose secret remained untold,
"Game to the point of bein' mad"
  The stockmen all avowed
Never a hope McGinty had
But he gave his life for the Irish lad
  His son, by Sally O'Dowd.

A Pot of Curry

"Five hundred head", the drover said
  to the English new-chum from Surrey
"Fattened out west where the grass is best
  "And they're all goin' into the Curry".

The new-chum gazed with face amazed
  As the drover lit up a durri
"No cooking pot would hold the lot
  Bai Jove, to make a curry".

Said the drover, "mate, they face their fate
  To feed both white man and murri
To-day they feast, each happy beast
  Tomorrow they land in the Curry".

And leaving the chum standing doubtful and dumb
  The drover, without any hurry
Attending his job slowly headed the mob
  Down the stock-route that led to Cloncurry.

NEIL PERCIVAL

Fading Hoofbeats

Silent the old stockyard tonight
   Neglected beyond repair
But under the moon's increasing light
   Comes a sound on the still night air.
Fading hoofbeats softly emerge
   From days of an era gone
Drummed is the bushman's final dirge
   But legends will linger on.

Legends of durable women and men
   Who battled famine and drought
Stories of faith and fortitude when
   The frontier was pushed far out
People who parried hardship's thrust
   Stubbornly standing their ground
Claimed by the years and gone to dust
   Where the fading hoofbeats sound.

Fading hoofbeats where stars look down
   On the ghosts of Australia's past
Echoing soft on the sandhill's crown
   And acres of blacksoil vast.
Over the ridges of box and pine
   West where the dust-wrack blows
North to the Queensland border line
   And south where the Murray flows.

Eastward by valley and frowning hill
   On tracks that were cold and long
Fading hoofbeats I hear you still
   At night when the memories throng.
The horseback men from days gone by
   Silent wraiths in the grass
Under the dome of midnight sky
   The fading hoofbeats pass.

Goaded by poverty's painful push
  In a limitless land far flung
They conquered the wide Australian bush
  And went to their graves unsung.
Gone to unmarked and unhallowed ground
  By progress pushed to the side
But at night when the fading hoofbeats sound
  Still in my heart they ride!

Discarded

The temperature soars as the sun beams hot
  As the fire of a blacksmith's welding
On arid expanses God forgot
Shunned by the Devil this starved-out spot
And shortly will lie in the mud to rot
  The bones of the old bay gelding.

See him plod through the burning dust
  A boney scaffolding lurching
To the shrinking waterhole's stagnant crust
Where death sits waiting with claws out-thrust
And high on the trees in evil lust
  The patient crows are perching.

A gambler's bauble now cast aside
  But a champion in days departed
Fawned on and feted with greedy pride
When gleaming and soft was his glossy hide
And strong his muscles and swift his stride
  When for money his strength was martyred.

At Randwick under the autumn skies
  To a thunder of hoofbeats ringing
How he stretched his neck for a golden prize
Round the turn and over the rise
Hearing the crowds' excited cries
  As the whips were wildly swinging.

Dumped in a paddock devoid of feed
  Where long have the drought-fiends loitered
Paying the price of a gamester's greed
Like honest creatures of human breed
Who similar much to a faithful steed
  Are by cunning and graft exploited.

A Droving Song

Roll the swags and pack the nags
  The rising river swells
Leave the hags and drunken jags
  Around the bush hotels.
One last shout, we're movin' out
  The open road's ahead
Have no doubt there's work about
  The idle days are dead.
Roll your spurs, the springtide stirs
  Forget the girls and wine
Time inters when man defers
  Turn the horses south from Condamine!

Streamlets gush through gullies lush
  Where hungry cattle wait
See them rush by yard and crush
  And every boundary gate.
Long and lank and lean of flank
  The travelling mobs are seen
By river bank. lagoon and tank
  They gorge on grasses green.
The dingo wails as dawning pales
  On beef he loves to dine
Climb the rails and twist their tales
  Head 'em down the road from Condamine!

Roan and red they slowly spread
  Baldy, black and white
Resting fed when day is dead
  And stars are winking white.
Drifting down the sandhill's crown
  Through rocks and stony shards

69

Border town and stock-route brown
   To southern slaughter yards.
With forceful pride the ringers ride
   In days of rain or shine
Casting wide when stragglers hide
   Goin' down the road from Condamine.

Take a seat and cop a treat
   The drover's scanty fare
Stringy meat is hard to eat
   But tired men never care
Damper hot that hits the spot
   Bundy rum as well
Drink a tot, then in the pot
   There's curry warm as hell.
Spread your rolls around the coals
   To sleep your minds consign
Weary souls with doubtful goals
   Goin' down the road from Condamine!

To an Old Riding Boot

Hard the upper cracked and worn
  Broken the elastic
Lost and lonely and forlorn
  In a world of plastic.
Relic from a bygone times
  Of romantic lustre
When in strength and pride sublime
  Ringers made the muster.

Memories come of early light
  When the east was greying
Red the camp-fire winking bright
  Horse-bells music playing.
Home the rolling pastures wide
  Free of regulation
Saddle up and careless ride
  No set destination.

Living only for the day,
  Timeless land beguiling
Grief and trouble far away
  Face them bold and smiling.
Youthful minds from ancient ways
  Modern lifestyles sever
Gone the times of stock and graze
  Departed now forever.

Down the final track we go
  Time's grim minions blight us
Fading sight and gouty toe
  Rheumatoid arthritis.
Sad old boot with spur-marks deep
  Causing recollection
Looking at you long I weep
  For lost youth's perfection.

71

The Darling Pea "Indigo"

On western plains in swooning heat
  Where devils make all gods retreat
And carrion birds the corpses eat
  There's lots of funny trees and plants
Well occupied by flies and ants
  And in their shade the swagman pants.

That is the place you'll daily see
  A legume called the Darling Pea
Not safe to take internally
  For when they eat it up, the stock
Like disco dancers shake and rock
  And stagger round and fall with shock.

You see, before Capone and Bugs
  Old Nature started pushing drugs
To hook the squatters' four-legged mugs.
  Purple and mauve the blossoms grow
Where turgid bore-drains slowly flow
  Old bushmen call it Indigo.

And when it seeds 'neath summer sky
  Horses and cattle all get high
And know not what and care not why.
  A gay exotic plant, it's true
But cold and deadly through and through
  Like brassy sheilas in the 'Loo.

The city drug squads long have sought
  To have the heroin pushers caught
Their efforts bold have come to naught.
  Perhaps they'll hear the squatters' plea
And seek with great alacrity
  The blokes who grow the Darling Pea.

72

Bloat

Where the sluggish Gwydir wanders
  'Neath the flats above each bank
When the winter rain was generous
  Grew the clover green and rank.
Though a rich and luscious fodder
  It was sorrowful to note
Now on cold and windy evenings
  It gave milking cows the bloat.

When the air with frost was laden
  In the waning afternoons
Time again we saw a milker
  Sides inflated like balloons
Paying dear for gormandizing
  All intestines overstrained
Swollen by the toxic gases
  That the clover-leaves contained.

Then her teeth would grind and rattle
  Like a tractor in the mud
As she tried with burps and belches
  To regurgitate the cud.
Useless cures old hands believed in
  (Lack of learning, I suppose)
"Get Stockholm tar to fix her"
  "Spinkle pepper on her nose".

"Get a pocket-knife and tap her"
  "Shove a hosepipe down her neck"
Hopeless methods all untested
  Thought to keep the bloat in check.
Then with eyeballs dull distended
  She would lean against a post

73

And with mournful sighs and bellows
  Painfully give up the ghost.

Soon an ancient motor-lorry
  To the scene would driven be
And the corpse dispatched behind it
  To the nearest fallen tree.
And the owner, quite remorseful
  To unkindly fate would bow
Muttering doleful imprecations
  As the flames engulfed his cow.

Now to-day the rural scientists
  Have dispelled our fears and hopes
By controlling bloat in cattle
  With the latest pills and dopes
And the hard times long have vanished
  When we slaved for every crust
And no more we have to worry
  If the milker mild might bust.

The Track
to Yesterday

Drop your load and rest, oh weary traveller
  See! the shades of night are falling fast
Take a trip along the track to yesterday.
  Dream again your dreams of seasons past.
Sitting where the camp-fire glows and glitters
  Still the sombre night and soft the rain
Looking back along the road to yesterday
  Living in rememberance joy and pain.

Thinking sad and glad of old romances
  When the fire of youth was burning strong
Empty words and soft deceitful glances
  Dreams that to a dying past belong.
Travelling once again the tracks of memory
  Grieving for a heart that wasn't true
Looking back along the road to yesterday
  Seeing all the things we didn't do.

Wishing we could live the old life over
  Back before the world was mean and small.
Endless lay the long leagues for the rover
  Where no longer now the Red Gods call.
Short and slow of step with faces haggard
  Far too late the bad mistakes to rue
Travelling down the track that leads to yesterday
  Mourning all the things we didn't do.

Fortune that escaped us, never mind it
  Fame we dreamed about and never gained.
Gleaners of the gold, who seldom find it
  Losers by the gods of luck disdained.

Looking back on days of tears and laughter
    Times of vibrant joy and cruel dismay
Hoping for a better life hereafter
    Dreaming on the track to yesterday.

Rest and dream with spells of memory binding
    Ageing minds as dreary day grows late
Take a tramp along the road to yesterday
    Where we held our tournaments with fate.
Live again the old desires long sleeping
    Scattered far along life's stony way
Ashes cold where flames of youth were leaping
    Landmarks on the track to yesterday.

76

The Bathurst Burr

Summer rain has brought it back
Biggest nuisance on the track
   Bushmen all concur
Foul and noxious indeed
Spreading its unwholesome seed
   The Bathurst Burr.

Chokes the herbage and the grass
Everywhere the stock must pass
   Sharp as any spur
Reaching out its claws to spoil
All the cultivated soil
   The Bathurst Burr.

Quite immune to modern sprays
Frenzied ploughing won't erase
   Poisons can't deter
On the fleeces it gathers thick
'Til the sheep to-gether stick.
   "Blast the burr!"

In the horses' tails and manes
Full ascendancy it gains.
   Any canine cur
With a silky coat and soft
Finds himself afflicted oft
   By the burr.

Bagmen drunk and camping late
By a lonely station gate
   When at dawn they stir

Find their blankets loaded down
With the little seedlings brown
   From the burr.

Of our weeds the greatest pest
Horticulturalists attest
   But it might deter
Pastoral public servants dumb
Who a bigger pest become
   Than the burr.

The Hand of Father Time

(Advice by an old shearer)

The shearin' is a tough affair
   A game that's quite misleadin'
Yer gamble drink and brook no care
   The future never heedin'.
Yer feel content when young and spry
   With the boggi in yer flipper
But when yer youth has passed yer by
   Life doesn't seem so chipper.
With pains and aches that come and go
   When winter days are colder
And the hand of Father Time yer know
   Is restin' on yer shoulder.

No longer can yer do yer stuff
   As when fires of youth were leapin'
And yer find the run ain't long enough
   To fit that extra sheep in.
When yer try to stay with some young bloke
   Who to cut a deuce is tryin'
And yer ain't got time to grab a smoke
   While the pressure he's applyin'.
When yer muscles ache with every blow
   And each day yer feelin' older
Then the hand of Father Time yer know
   Is restin' on yer shoulder.

So take my tip and save a quid
   For poverty ain't funny
You'll regret the foolish things yer did
   When yer've squandered all yer money.

When the future offers naught but strain
  And the toil to earn a deener
And the young coves make yer drag the chain
  'Til yer frame grows poor and leaner.
When yer livin' standard ain't sublime
  And yer health begins to moulder
Then yer know the hand of Father Time
  Is restin' on yer shoulder.

The Rough Sheds
West of the Darling

They say it's a land that's made of sand
  Made of sand
  Made of sand
Where the rum-sodden ringers get out of hand
And the starving bagmen take command
From the discouraged squatters who own the land
  'Neath the rough sheds west of the Darling.

The shearers grizzle both day and night
  Day and night
  Day and night
And they drink cheap plonk with a mad delight
'Til they shiver and spew and shake with fright
And scream with the horror sandy blight
  At the rough sheds west of the Darling.

The bloated rouseabouts helpless lie
  Helpless lie
  Helpless lie
When they gorge like goannas on mutton pie
And they groan with guts-ache and want to die
While the greasy crows sit hopefully by
  At the rough sheds west of the Darling.

There's many a dead-beat got the sack
  Got the sack
  Got the sack
And staggered away on a furnace track
Where he couldn't withstand the heat's attack
Now his bones are bleached and he won't be back
  To the rough sheds west of the Darling.

The crazy hatters are hard as hogs
  Hard as hogs
  Hard as hogs
And they sleep all day by a fire of logs
And their matted beards are a home for wogs
And they end up food for the native dogs
  At the rough sheds west of the Darling.

The mirage flaunts its phantom lake
  Phantom lake
  Phantom lake
Promoting a thirst you never can slake
And it swallows you up like a carpet snake
On the merciless sand where the lizards bake
  Near the rough sheds west of the Darling.

It's a far, far cry from civilised homes
  Civilised homes
  Civilised homes
But adventurous man unchallenged roams
So next week I'm packin' me cutters and combs
And soon you'll hear of me writin' poems
  At the rough sheds west of the Darling.

Glencoe
Rodeo

At the town of Glencoe where the stringy barks grow
Stands a newly-built rodeo yard
Where each wild mountain boy must great courage employ
When for fortune and fame riding hard.
Every half-broken colt that can strike, buck or bolt
Will be mustered in early New Year
To provide special thrills as the riders take spills
Soaring high in the New England air.

They need lots of good luck when the big Brahmas buck
Few riders get on them to stay
But their sorrows are drowned, for the rodeo ground
From the pub is a half-mile away.
So for those who can't ride lots of beer is supplied
'Neath the hills crowned in winter with snow
If you've money to spend I can quite recommend
A day of good sport at Glencoe.

There's a big dance at night in the moon's mellow light
All the sheilas are friendly and true
If you can't win a heart, in the feasting take part
On the steaks at the big barbecue.
Put a knot in your swag, throw some grub in a bag
Then off to New England you go
Where welcome you'll be and wild sport you will see
With hospitable folk at Glencoe.

NEIL PERCIVAL

Finishing On

A dashing punter bought a horse
   In hopes to win a pile
But in every start he gave the beast
   It didn't show much style.
"He finished on", the trainer said,
   "He's still a bit too stout
Next start he looks a livin' cert
   To take the money out".

"I put a packet on him"
   Said the punter, looking sad
"That's three times now I've backed him
   Using every cent I had".
"But he finished on", the trainer smiled
   "He's very near the dough
Next start he looks a real good thing
   So have another go"

Next start he was a cert declared
   By every tout and con.
But still behind another horse
   He bravely finished on.
The punter game kept backing up
   But the horse's doom was sealed
In every start he finished on
   Behind a tiring field.

"A longer race", the trainer said
   "He isn't bred for speed"
Again the cuddy finished on
   But well back from the lead.
The owner mortgaged all he had
   For a final desperate punt

The gallant horse still finished on
   But didn't hit the front.

So to the knacker's yard he went
   An ending rude and rough
The brutal fate for every horse
   That can't go quick enough.
The bookies, showing profit great
   Gave thanks with heart and soul
And the dashing punter finished on....
   He finished ON THE DOLE.

Not Now!

("Even the bloody dogs won't work in Australia to-day". Remark by a grazier friend of the author.")

The squatter sat on a coolibah log
   Too weary even for talking
With a knocked-up horse and a sore-footed dog
   And the lead of the sheep were walking.
"Go back! Go back! to the dog he said
   Go round 'em and kick up a row"
But the cunning old kelpie shook his head
   And said, "Not now! Not now!"
"I'm not goin' to say "bow-wow".

"Long have I toiled 'til my feet were sore
   On sandridge and swamp and plain
But times have changed and I'll work no more
   So the graziers gold may gain".

"You useless bastard", the squatter swore
   You break a man's heart and soul
The lazy son of a canine whore
   You're worse than the blokes on the dole
Or the loafers who work in a Government job
   Don't tell me "not now, not now"
Go get yourself up to the lead of the mob
   And tell the hoggets "bow wow".
I want you to say "bow wow".

But the kelpie remembered the working class
   Who for years were underpaid
And he shook his head and sat on his arse
   And never a move he made.
He smirked as the squatter with rage turned grey
   And said "I will not kow-tow"

For the working dogs in Australia to-day
No longer need say "bow wow".
Not now, not now.
Imperial power has lost all sway
And we don't have to say "bow wow".

NEIL PERCIVAL

Wild Pigs
Running

Out where the blacksoil plains are stark
   Grisly gleaners of lost men's lives
By lonely homsteads where watch-dogs bark
At shadowy shapes in the dreary dark
   The wary wild pig survives.
Watch them trotting at early dawn
   to the stagnant lagoons to feed
Their sustenance small from the sags is torn
Where the curlew's voice is a cry forlorn
   And the shag and the wild-duck breed.

Lying submerged through the noontide hour
   Gaunt sows and cute suckers small
Battered old boars determined and dour
Sprawling asleep in the lignum sour
   Or under green gum-trees tall.
Wary of hunter or hunting hound
   In the waterways cool they hide
Where red-bellied snakes and frogs are found
The wild pig relishes sodden ground
   'Til the swamps by the drought are dried.

Then ever westward they make their way
   Down the slowly receding streams
Over sandhills red where the brolgas play
And the old buck possum grizzled and grey
   In the spout of a dead tree dreams.
When the big rains fall the migration ends
   And no longer the grunters roam
Returning quickly as Nature sends
Her message old where the channel wends
   It's way through their watery home.

Pioneerin'
Australia
(A plea for equality)

That's where Rafferty died, they say
Got off the track and lost his way
    Pioneerin' Australia
Left his life on the blacksoil vast
God only knows where his bones are cast
Shearer man with a dubious past
    Pioneerin' Australia

Up on that ridge where the bloodwoods grow
That's where they buried Liverpool Joe
    Pioneerin' Australia
Crushed to death be a fallin' tree
On poverty pay for an absentee
It coulda bin you or it coulda bin me
    Pioneerin' Australia

See that waterhole below the rise
That's where a bonded servant lies
    Costly failure
Fell in and drowned where the water was deep
Tryin' to rescue the master's sheep
Tucker was lackin' and labour was cheap
    Pioneerin' Australia.

Old hands tell yer in early days
Fellers died in the bushfires' blaze
    Pioneerin' Australia
Well I remember Dinny McGuire
Overcome be the heat of the fire
All we could do was watch him expire
    Pioneerin' Australia.

In the papers you've often read it
How wealthy people get all the credit
    For pioneerin' Australia
What about all the workin' classes?
Whose graves are lost in the weeds and grasses
Sons of the lags who got kicked in the asses
    Pioneerin' Australia.

Over on the Dry Side

("It's the hardest, most God-forsaken place on earth, full of dead-beats and petty crims. But out there west of the Paroo, over on the dry side, there's a bloody lot of freedom from piddlin' little laws and regulations".... Remarked to the author by an old hand from the far west of Queensland.)

Over on the dry side
That's where the ghosts at night ride
   West of Louth and Bourke
That's where the ringers have greenhide thews
And stomachs of brass to repel the booze
And there's little to gain and less to lose
   Over on the dry side
   That's where the devils lurk.

Over on the dry side
That's where the ghostly ghouls glide
   That's where the drought-fires burn
Where brains are addled and hearts are broke
And the hell-fiends caper on sands that smoke
And a winding-sheet is the dust-storm's cloak
   Over on the dry side
   Country of no return.

Over on the dry side
That's where misfortune's high tide
   Beaches the wrecks of life
Living a dead past down unfearing
Lustful and loveless, lewd and uncaring
Callous their creed, no conscience bearing
   Over on the dry side
   Soldiers of storm and strife.

Over on the dry side
That's where the lost souls fly wide
　Searching for peace unfound
Seeking the hand of God unbidden
Nameless graves by the sand-drift hidden
Freed of sins and of troubles ridden
　Over on the dry side
　Sheathed in unhallowed ground.

Over on the dry side
That's where the wanted men hide
　Freedom in woe and pain
Hard, but freedom never the less
Far from the modern civilised mess
And the Red Gods call me I must confess
　Over to the dry side
　I would return again.

The Same Result

The squatter rich to Darwin went
 A man who did himself well
A Northern playboy on pleasure bent
He booked his lodging with great content
 At the township's leading hotel.
He dined on lobster and champagne light
 In a restaurant gleaming and grand
Expensive cigars and napkins white
'Twas a wonderful scene in splendour bright
 With music played by a band.
Then swiftly a taxi hied him away
 To the mansion shining and bright
Of a ravishing wanton who earned high pay
Her sins were dark in the light of day
 But her charms were great by night.

A ringer uncouth to Darwin rode
 He was ragged and rough and poor
A skeleton steed his legs bestode
And he visioned the crude bamboo abode
 Of a yellow Eurasian whore.
A meal he prepared from stale corn meat
 Damper and vile black tea
Sweating in Capricorn's humid heat
While cicadas drummed a depressing beat
 And the frogs croaked a melodee.
Then he went, forgetting worry and toil
 To the shack where his love awaited
Her efforts earned her no golden spoil
Unwashed, but greased with coconut oil
 His longing she quickly sated.

Now can you tell me, my readers kind
 If my verse you are closely attending
Did the squatter greater enjoyment find
Than the ringer to hardship long resigned
 And with limited coin for spending?

NEIL PERCIVAL

The Shorthorns

White or dappled or red as flame
From the hills of Durham the shorthorns came
  Over the salt seas wide
To the timeless country a world away
Where the brigalows glitter silvery grey
  And the world's best stockmen ride.

Selective breeding the strain improved
Slowly inland the big mobs moved
  Under the dust-wrack brown
With quality constant in every line
On runs from the Gulf to Condamine
  The shorthorn won renown.

Down where the Snowy runs deep and dark
By Monaro mountains cold and stark
  Where wombats make their home
Or where western rivers wend their way
Under the gums on a summer day
  The placid shorthorns roam.

Shiny and sleek from springtide graze
On Queensland pastures by lonely ways
  Where Warrigal lurks unseen
Watch them fatten where foothills rise
Switching their tails at the countless flies
  That swarm from the verdure green.

Strong resistance to blight and pest
Veterinary officers all attest
  Temperament calm and bland
Showing the way where weight prevails
When butchered carcasses hit the scales
  For export to foreign land.

Over the plain at fall of night
Ghostly hulks in the fading light
   They move from the scrub to feed
Many a nation starved for beef
Has cause to thank with profound relief
   The famous shorthorn breed.

The Death Bone

On, the *moppingarra points the bone to-day
So be sure nobody gets in the way
    For the deadly effects of this evil charm
    Can freeze or bury, burn or embalm
    Somebody's headed for a heap of harm
When the moppingarra points the bone.

Skinny and dark and elongated
By desert temperatures dehydrated
    He sits near a rock on the sandhill's crest
    With tribal scars on his arms and chest
    And the pitiful victim will find no rest
When the moppingarra points the bone.

In a sacred bag made of paper-bark
The bone lies hidden in a cavern dark
    The terrible bone that can curse and kill
    Cure your sickness or make you ill
    And devil-devils prowl when the night is still
If the moppingarra points the bone.

In the spectral light of the Territory moon
He silent sneaks in Kaditcha shoon
    While the tribesmen shiver in wurlies dark
    And hide their heads under sheets of bark
    Lest the spirit-men leave them stiff and stark
When the moppingarra points the bone.

But the moppingarra's prestige is small to-day

He's just an old murri who gets in the way
   Of the terrible bone that scientists wield
   To its nuclear magic mankind must yield
   And the fate of the world could be shortly sealed
If the white man points the bone.

                    *Moppingarra....
                    A witch-doctor of the
                    West Australian
                    Aboriginal tribes.

The Shed Expert

In sheds where hardship close attends
   Where Western tracks are windin'
I tell yer mate, a lot depends
   On the bloke who does the grindin'.
Yer often find a lazy nark
   Who'll never change the emery
It's too worn out to raise a spark
   And so he grinds from memory.
There's blokes who use a heavy fist
   Til yer tools are burned and singein'
To push and shove they can't resist
   'Til they nearly stop the engine.

There's fireworks fans who rasp away
   'Til showers of sparks are blindin'
Look mate, yer don't find every day
   A cove can do the grindin'.
The greasy cook's an awful sight
   By whiskey spiflicated
The squatter is so bloody tight
   He's always constipated.
Yer pen-mate always seems to find
   A foolproof way to snob yer
Contractors have one thought in mind
   The quickest way to rob yer.

The penner-up gets drunk and sad
   Complaint he's always findin'
But none of these can drive yer mad
   Like a mug who does the grindin'.
Experts at what? I'd like to know
   The shearer moans and mutters

And putrid lauguage starts to flow
    When he sees his combs and cutters
Ruined and burned; in such a state
    It drives a feller dizzy
"Let's drown this crude imposter, mate
    An expert!! Just where is he".

He's with us somewhere, I suppose
    He takes a lot of findin'
The skilful bloke who really knows
    The way to do the grindin'.

The Synthetic Rider

(Told by an old bushman)

I'll sing yer a song about a bloke
   That follers the rodeos
He fills yer ears with his horrible croak
'Til yer temper boils and yer heart gets broke
And every cowboy he's sure to provoke
   Tellin' him how to ride
   Tellin' him how to ride

Yer see him comin' out of the bar
   He never comes out of the chute
The bloke who dreams he's a show-ring star
Wherever the buckin' horses are
He couldn't sit in a motor car
   But he tells yer how to ride.
   He tells yer how to ride.

Yer find him at every rodeo
   He's never too far away
Should storm-clouds gather or drought-winds blow
He'll be there skitin' come rain or snow
Yer never see him havin' a go
   But he tells yer how to ride.
   He tells yer how to ride.

If yer ask him to have a try
   He's always got some complaint
A broken leg or a bungy eye
A misplaced rib or a damaged thigh
But he keeps hangin' round, I don't know why
   And he tells yer how to ride
   He tells yer how to ride.

How he exists is hard to say
   Perhaps he's only a bum
Cadgin' his drinks from day to day
Givin' no thought to payin' his way
Loudly and noisily havin' his say
   Tellin' yer how to ride
   Tellin' yer how to ride.

One of these days a buckin' horse
   Or maybe a Brahma bull
Will land on the bludger with terrible force
There's no one will feel the slightest remorse
And he'll pass away still yappin', of course
   Tellin' yer how to ride
   Tellin' yer how to ride.

And when he goes up where the saints belong
   Forgiven for all his sins
He'll bash the lugs of the cherubic throng
And if Matthew and Mark come trottin' along
On Heavenly donkeys stout and strong
   He'll be tellin' 'em how to ride
   Tellin' 'em how to ride.

The Ghost Riders

Darkness falls on a rodeo ending
  A day of excitement and thrills
And contestants mistakes are defending
  Quite regardless of bruises and spills
No Brahma or saddle-bronc fearing
  Never heeding the moment of truth
Riding wild, unafraid and uncaring
  With the reckless demeanour of youth.

And I wonder, as memories come wending
  Through the dust of a past that has gone
Were the ghosts of old riders attending
  From a faraway yard looking on
Where the trees on the Jordan are shady
  Under heavenly mountain and ridge
Were you watching us, Boomerang Brady
  Were you cheering our efforts, Ben Bridge?

Old man Skuthorpe would have to be present
  To relive all his days that were great
And in style both flamboyant and pleasant
  Comes the Queenslander, dark Billy Waite,
To the bar where the champions palaver
  All excitement when fortune has smiled
Are you knocking a beer down, Bill Carver
  Are you buckling the spurs, Charley Wilde?

For a spell Billy Timmins may tarry
  And his presence is sure to be felt
Plus the Englishman known as Wild Harry
  Who lies buried on Africa's veld.

Many more of renown I could mention
   Though for long years departed they are
How comparing their skills caused dissension
   In discussions at showground and bar.

In their day they were fearless and famous
   Still their legendary feats linger on
Soon the short years that claimed them will claim us
   And the pride of our youth will be gone.
So good luck every rodeo rival
   And a toast to the hard life we know
At the end of our earthly survival
   May we go where the ghost riders go.
   May we go where the ghost riders go!!

To an Old Stockman

On a bench 'neath a tall pepperina
   at a pub on the track farther out
Flat broke, in his kick not a deener
   not the price of a meal or a shout
Sat an old stockman weary and broken,
   a relic of years now long gone
With his thoughts of a past life unspoken
   he relaxed in the sun, dreaming on.

With acclaim from no writer or singer,
   no awards, no publicity won,
Dream your dreams of a lost youth, old ringer,
   dream your dreams as you drowse in the sun
Dream again of that youth long departed
   for small gain, at the rich man's behest
When the strength of your young years was bartered
   on the old mustering camps farther west.

Saffron sunrise when saltbush would shimmer
   as contented the big bullocks fed
Shadowed evenings when bright was the glimmer
   of the stars winking white overhead.
Sudden stampedes when blacksoil was slippery
   from the rain as the storm-tempest swells,
The dash to the beach at Gallipoli,
   the slope to the grim Dardanelles.

Gulf country where dark people wandered,
   dry deserts where dust-devils flew
Grog-shanties where hard cash was squandered,
   loose women whose scruples were few.

A bush girl, of true love the bringer,
   departed with sad heart unwon
Dream your dreams of a lost youth, old ringer,
   dream your dreams as you drowse in the sun.

Hard spills in the yard gamely taken,
   the hazards of perilous trade
Rough men by society forsaken,
   unacknowledged, a strong hand they played
In the labour lists winning a nation
   while the rich man the plaudits received,
Hard propounders of hard occupation
   departing unsung and ungrieved.

Just a few like yourself still remaining,
   battling on be there sunshine or rain
Still accepting, with heart uncomplaining
   God's bounty of pleasure and pain.
No scribe to proclaim them, no singer,
   travelling slow in a race nearly run
Dream your dreams of a lost youth, old ringer,
   dream your dreams as you drowse in the sun.

Day to Day
(The ringers' creed)

Belt of timber endless seeming
   Emerald kruis, brigalows grey
Bush birds strike uneven chorus
   Heralding the breaking day.
Bright above the lightening scrub-line
   Swift the sunbeams breaking through
Silhouette the darkened tree-tops
   Still and stark against the blue.

In the bend the bells are clanking
   Where the dewy grasses quake
Slow the Muckadilla trickles
   Fluid and silent as a snake.
Head the horses west for Mitchell
   Crude diversions wait us there
Lamplight gay where glasses glitter
   And for some a heart held dear.

Leaving for a while behind us
   Weary days of care and toil
Starry nights hold spells to bind us
   While we watch the billy boil.
Games of chance and grog unending
   'Til the cheques go down the drain
Needless shouts and reckless spending
   Then it s saddle up again.

Down life's stock-route careless drifting
   Where the miles are spaced in years
Sands of time forever shifting
   Soon will bury doubts and fears.
Hard rough men ambition lacking
   Satisfied with pittance pay

110

Wasted lives like muffled hoofbeats
  Slowly fade and fade away.

Ponder not, oh ringers weary
  Leave your future to the fates
Head the horses west to Mitchell
  Where a small diversion waits.
Life and laughter calls the rover
  Heed not what the gods attest
Live from day to day, bold drover
  Head the horses to the west!

Old Time

(Told by an old rodeo star.)

The rodeo is in full stride
   And round the dusty yard
The hopeful ringers wait to ride
   With reckless disregard.
With confidence and nerve sublime
   All dangerous risk they spurn
But that grand old buckin' horse called Time
   Is waitin' for HIS turn.

I've watched 'em come and watched 'em go
   For many seasons now
The top dogs of the rodeo
   With laurels on the brow.
Resplendant in their youth and strength
   They seek the winner's crown
And gamely go to any length
   To tame an outlaw down.

With shinin' spurs and Stetson hat
   They sing and dance and shout
But never seem to notice that
   The years are runnin' out.
They drink and love with ardent force
   And careless spend the loot
While Time, that tough old buckin' horse
   Is waitin' in the chute.

He's waitin' patient to attend
   To champs from near and far
And he always throws 'em in the end
   No matter who they are.
You see old riders crippled sad
   Burred up and stony broke

112

But Time's still in there buckin' bad
    And thinks it's all a joke.

Champions once strong, who now are weak
    Worn out in heart and soul
They're hobblin' up the street to seek
    The pension or the dole.
The has-beens lost, with no resource
    They pass in dull despair
But Time, that ageless buckin' horse
    He ALWAYS will be there.

He never tires or packs it in
    Or fails to do his best
He knows for sure he's goin' to win
    As the records all attest.
So skilful riders in your prime
    An ear to wisdom lend
The tough old buckin' horse called Time
    Will throw you in the end.

Bull in the Bedourie

Gentle listeners hear my story
About bull in the bedourie
    On the cattle camps where ride the ringers bold
When the stolen beef is grilling
Each bedouri oven filling
    At the camp-fire every night as yarns are told.
Now Diamantina Danny
Was a duffer cool and canny
    Made a living stealing cattle night and day
Until the stock-squad tricky
Caught him with a slaughtered mickey
    And the stern old sergeant heard the ringer say
"Throw a bit of bull in the bedouri
"Sit her where the brigalow ashes glow
    "Carve the rump for slices fat and gory
    "Let me fill me tank before I go.

"Let me feast before I face the jury
"Grab the Whitely King and bull the tea
    "Throw a bit of bull in the bedouri
    "Seems I've made a date with destinee-e.

But bewildered were the coppers
And they soon put on the stoppers
    When a brand upon the hide they couldn't find
Said the sergeant, "on this vealer
Is no mark to prove a stealer
    So I fear to jail he cannot be consigned".
And he put up book and texta
While the duffer flashed his dexter
    Said, "you nearly gave me failure of the heart

114

"Now your hopes are gone to glory
"Throw some bull in the bedouri
And try a juicy steak ere you depart."

"Curb your temper mounting to a fury
Show a smile to hide your sad dismay
    Throw a bit of bull in the bedouri
    Wait the chance to win another day.
    So the sergeant brave departed
    Back again to where he started
With a look of sad frustration on his face
    Sure the brand was carefully hidden
    Ere the stock-squad came unbidden
And they didn't ever guess the hiding-place.
    It was planted red and gory
    'Neath a steak in the bedouri
Slowly turning to a sizzled piece of hide
    And the plant remains a mystery
    For the stockmen's tricks are history
In the outback where the cattle-duffers ride.
    So throw a bit of bull to blind the jury
    And soften up the judge's stony glare
    Always bull to put in the bedouri
    Saddle up and ride without a care.

Throw a juicy cut in the bedouri
Bonzer grub that beats the prison fare.

NEIL PERCIVAL

Stock-Camp Memories

Beside the stockwhip's greenhide coil
  My spurs hang draped with dust
Reminder of the days of toil
  To earn a scanty crust.
Where ringers tough their calling plied
  On horses hard and lean
Oft contemplating wealth denied
  And men they might have been.
The tide of youth comes flooding back
  By memory deeply etched
Of every lonely droving track
  On endless acres stretched.

I see the white of winter frosts
  The gleam of summer suns
The tree-tops by wild storm winds tossed
  On distant Western runs.
The big gaunt steers by thirst impelled
  Where grass was scarce and dead
The leaders slobbering when they smelled
  The waterholes ahead.
The shandy bars where grog was vile
  And bums made sad beseech
The barmaids dressed in garish style
  Brash roses out of reach.

Droll and undaunted, tried and true
  My old mates silent pass
Frustration and denial they knew
  Hard men of working class.

Weird tales they told devoid of truth
  Where camp-fires flickered red
Old stories tall that like my youth
  In time's grey mists have fled.
But oft at night when fancy stirs
  And lost desires detain
I don once more the dusty spurs
  And ride down memory's lane.

NEIL PERCIVAL

The Modern Ringer

Where Marlborough country danger hides
　　Unhurried, unafraid
The modern ringer boldly rides
　　And smokes a tailor-made.
It isn't very long ago
　　That this new type appeared
His small transistor radio
　　Howls pop tunes wild and weird.

He sits his metal mount with ease
　　And strokes its shining frame
Constructed by the Japanese
　　It grows not tired or lame.
Of spur or whip he has no need
　　These to the past belong
He blows the horn to turn the lead
　　Or push the tail along.

The old bush blokes seem out of place
　　Beside this gilded chap
To shield his pale and vacant face
　　He wears a baseball cap.
He never seems to sweat or pant
　　Beneath the sun's hot glare
His underarm deodorant
　　Rides with his can of beer.

For him no flannel sour and damp
　　No dirty dungarees
But T-Shirt with a foreign stamp
　　And shorts above the knees.

In branding yards his thongs are neat
    Cool apparel that suits
For cowdung washes off bare feet
    Much easier than boots.

And should our hero feel unwell
    And lose the track at night
His two-way radio will tell
    The homestead of his plight.
His dwelling is a classy place
    Where after eating tea
He watches J.R. Ewing chase
    The sheilas on T.V.

At nine A.M. he leaves the bunk
    To breakfast on the best
No damper stale or hard corn junk....
    French fries and chicken breast.
Kind Union benefits bestowed
    Protect him from the sack
Or the boss would send him down the road
    And get the old hands back.

The horseback men forever gone
    From every outback run
Who made the land and carried on
    Until the job was done.

We Came
To Ride
(or the Rodeo Code)

We arrive, and the trip wasn't easy
   But the day may provide better luck
See the saddle-broncs wild and uneasy
   And a pen full of bulls that can buck,
Dry the earth in the dusty arena
   Cracked and broken the rails of the yard
All our finances down to a deener
   And the sponsors show little regard
For the riders at hard risk competing
   In a game testing courage and skill
With fond hopes of success slowly fleeting
   But we came here to ride, and we will.

From the gulf to Victoria's border
   Roam the rodeo boys hunting fame
In a sport where hard knocks are the order
   For our art gaining little acclaim
By no lackey or servant attended
   No fortune aglitter the prize
In the red dirt of Queensland upended
   Or under Monaro's grey skies.
In the pubs seeking smiles from the charmers
   Loving lustful 'neath stars white and chill
On the morrow we tackle the Brahmas
   For we came here to ride, and we will.

Swarming hopeful like bees to the honey
   With no time to regret or to rue
There's the Timmins boys out for the money
   And Wakeman and Watts riding too.
Hoping hard as the judge gives the signal
   Listening long for the sound of the bell

In the camp-draft good fortune, Alf Bignell
  Good luck Peter Manchee as well.
Have a whiskey to keep your nerves steady
  Gulp it down as you fasten your eyes
On the bronc in the chute saddled ready
  How the liquor fresh courage supplies.
Watch the bay with the blaze, he's a fighter
  Grab the rope on his head, hold him still
While I get the girth up a bit tighter
  We came here to ride and we will.

To the bar, cheerful winners, sad losers
  Let us hope for things better to come
Ease the pain of sore bumps and bad bruises
  With a big dose of Bundaberg rum.
That's enough, better put on the stoppers
  Get a taxi to take us away
If we tangle to-night with the coppers
  We won't be competing next day.
In the show-ground the camp-fires are glowing
  By the swags spread for overtired souls
There's a drop of good liquor still flowing
  And some bull-meat grilled hot on the coals.
Slumber deep without sadness or sorrow
  And our dreams we perhaps may fulfil
There's a chance for the losers tomorrow
  We came here to ride, AND WE WILL!!

The Old Rider

See him at the stockyard standing
   Broken by the years and grey
Hands of time their share demanding
   Rider old who had his day.
Thinking back to joys departed
   When the buckers dipped and swung
Following his trade stout-hearted
   Now for him no songs are sung.
On top at every exhibition
   Long ago he showed them how
A rider in the great tradition
   By the fans forgotten now.

By no dangerous outlaw daunted
   Riding reckless high and wide
When the strength of youth he flaunted
   Fearless in his power and pride.
Always near the major prizes
   Always in the final round
Where the cloying dust cloud rises
   Red above the trampled ground.
Fame and fortune fair his mission
   Seeking every goal unwon
A rider in the great tradition
   Underneath the Western sun.

Foremost where the bright lights flicker
   Gay the girls and sweet the song
Yielding more and more to liquor
   Weak he grows who once was strong.
Nerves afire and frayed by tension
   Falls that on the system wear

Heading for a burned-out pension
   Sinking without thought or care.
Living free of inhibition
   Loving long and drinking late
A rider in the great tradition
   Buffeted by winds of fate.

Waistline hard before, now bloated
   Gone the will to ride at last
Courage by the grape promoted
   Shadows of the end descending fast
Memories of a wild past fading
   When with faultless skill he rode
Bearded cheeks and rags degrading
   Travelling dereliction's road.
Lost forever bold ambition
   Dreams of golden prizes won
A rider in the great tradition
   By the reckless years undone.

NEIL PERCIVAL

A Shearing Song

Time to pack the bag up
Time to roll the swag up
Hit the track, the Western sheds are done
Time that we were flyin'
Where the snows are dyin'
Meltin' in the pale September sun.
Where the skies are leaden
Down below the Weddin
Southward bound by Yass and Bribaree
Rollin' down to Cooma
Full of beer and humour
Rouseabouts and shearers on the spree.
CHORUS....
Rollin' down to Cooma
Rollin' down to Cooma
Rollin' down along the Southern line
Spring is comin' nearer
Callin' every shearer
Rollin' down to frosty Jindabyne
rollin' down to frosty Jindabyne.

All you guns and learners
Bums and money earners
Grab yer slender swags and catch the train
Rugged spur and valley
Hut and kitchen galley
Southern sheds are startin' once again.
Heed no idle rumour
There'll be work at Cooma
Men to fill the gaps on every board
Join us friend and neighbour
Southward lies the labour

127

Money for each willin' hand assured.
CHORUS....
   Rollin' down to Cooma
   Rollin' down to Cooma
Warm the days as winter snows decline
   Spring is drawin' nearer
   Callin' every shearer
To the frosty hills of Jindabyne.
To the frosty hills of Jindabyne.

   Where the sheep are small toys
   And the trees are tall, boys
Room for both the snagger and the gun
   Load the lizard tight, boys
   Set the tension light, boys
Put yer sights on forty every run.
   Shearers make no bloomer
   Now's the time at Cooma
If you want a wallet full of dough
   Meet a former stand-mate
   Truest in the land, mate
Fortune's waitin', hoist the swag and go
    CHORUS....
   Rollin' down to Cooma
   Rollin' down to Cooma
Shearers full of confidence and wine
   Belly-wools and fleeces
   Second cuts and pieces
On the frosty hill at Jindabyne
Frosty Southern hills at Jindabyne.

128

Ballad of the
Dancing Googar

He stood beside a ti-tree clump
  Where the Beardy slowly flows
The feral scent of native dogs.
  Was heavy on his clothes.
A tough old scalper grim and grey
  Sad ghost of yesteryear
And his face displayed complete disgust
  When I offered him a beer.

"Dishwater, mate! That's all it is
  Worse'n a pail of slops
But I'll take a glass of Irish stout
  It REALLY wets yer chops
And often has a queer effect
  On the blokes who drink too quick
Now I mind the time I had me camp
  In the hills near Yarrowick.

"I'm sittin' in the tent one day
  Just off a drinkin' bout
Enjoyin' as a pick-me-up
  A glass of Irish stout,
When I hears a muffled footstep
  And I looks up to see
A big goanna standin' there
  And gazin' hard at me.

"A bowler hat was on his head
  A broadcloth suit he wore
And a little pipe of cherrywood
  Was juttin' from his jaw.

He spots the bottle in me hand
  And gestures with his snout
I grabs a pint and quickly pours
  A liberal measure out.

He put it down with one quick gulp
  And I can tell yer, boy
That a glow came to his scaley cheeks
  And his eyes lit up with joy.
I poured him out another one
  And it didn't hit the deck
He trembled as that bonzer drink
  Slid down his leathery neck.

"They say a reptile's blood is cold
  Of this I've got no doubt
But that old googar soon grew hot
  When he drank that Irish stout.
He ups and starts to sing and dance
  He did, upon me soul
With a style as neat as Fred Astaire
  He performed a rock 'n' roll.

"With rattlin' claws he soon displayed
  A groovey beat intense
Just like a modern teen-ager
  But the googar had more sense.
He grabbed the bottle from me hand
  And had another swig
Then round and round the tent he goes
  In a lively Irish jig.

"Until he bumped against the pole
  And knocked it out of plumb
And down upon me achin' head
  The whole damn shebang come.
When I came round and got me wits
  Me dancin' mate was gone

130

But in me ears his melody
    At times still lingers on.

"So now me tale is told, young man
    It's up to you to shout
Yer can have yer pint of watery beer
    But mine's an Irish stout.
If I drink it quick perhaps I'll see
    Before it knocks me flat
That spry old googar dancin'
    In his suit and bowler hat.

              ("Googar"....
              Aboriginal term for goanna.)

The Vengeance of Dingo Deparde

Doyen of doggers was "Dingo" Deparde
  poison and traps were his forte
Cruel practitioner pledged to provide
  a living in hardship wrought
For a wife and family he seldom saw
  as he roamed the Territory's waste
With a sulky and horse for his transport;
  he moved without hurry or haste.
Travelling alone in a barbaric land
  trusting no man black or white
Alert as the native dogs he sought
  in the dark of the desert night.

Close by a gum-girt waterhole
  he pitched his camp one day
And hidden deep in the shadowy clump
  six ochre-daubed myalls lay.
Warriors wild of the Brinken tribe
  with spear-points polished and hard
They craved the supplies they knew were stored
  in the camp of Dingo Deparde.
Their's for the taking, a royal feast
  when the lonely dogger was killed
Sugar and coffee, flour and salt,
  soon would their stomachs be filled.

The dogger's rifle stood by a tree
  as he knelt by the water green
And he charged his billy and drank his fill
  while the warriors waited unseen.
The spear that entered Dingo's ribs
  was flighted and flung full well

133

Startled and shocked to his feet he sprang,
   then mortally stricken he fell.
But he reached the rifle and fired a shot
   as the life-blood dripped from his side
And the confident charge of the myalls broke,
   in the cover they scattered to hide.

Pain-wracked and dizzy the dogger crawled
   in his tent on the open ground
Knowing his number was sure to go up
   'ere the hands of the clock went round
Knowing the myalls were certain to come
   for the food that the camp contained
Patiently waiting the plunder to seek
   when the life of their victim waned.
And Dingo thought of the children and wife
   that he never would see again
The lust for revenge on the Brinken men
   was a furnace that flamed in his brain.

Aloud he said, "It's the tucker they want,
   so I'll leave 'em a bloody fine feed
A banquet to fill their guts with fire,
   the last one they'll ever need.
"I'm bleedin' bad and I haven't got long
   but I still hold a bloody strong card
So I'll give the bludgers cause to regret
   that they ever saw Dingo Deparde".

He reached for the dirty calico bag
   that hung from the pole of the tent
And the small blue bottles his hand drew forth
   a smile to his features lent.

A wearying week went dragging by
   'ere a trooper came to the spot

And the stench of death was a sickening thing
　　for the days and nights had been hot.
Bloated and foul was the dogger's corpse
　　where the crows made clamorous row
And the deadly blue bottles lay close at hand
　　empty and harmless now.
The policeman went from the ransacked tent
　　to the waterhole green and wide
Six Brinken warriors lay at it's edge,
　　men who in agony died.

Swollen and rotting and ravaged they were
　　with faces twisted and hard
And the little blue bottles the story told
　　of the vengeance of Dingo Deparde.

Part and Parcel

Take a trip out back, young fellow
When the days of spring are mellow
Roll your bluey up and kiss your girl good-bye
  Feel no sorrow at departing
  For the rodeos are starting
And adventure waits for you my lad, beneath the Western Sky.
  When you hear the clamour rising
  Wild excitement advertising
See the dust of the arena, drifting slow
  Under summer suns that redden
  Or the rain-clouds rolling leaden
Well then my friend you'll know....
  My friend you'll know...
  That you're part and parcel of the rodeo.

Where the saddle-broncs are kicking
  At the riders bent on sticking
Spurring wildly high and wide in hopes to score
  All intent to prove perfection
  'Til they take up a selection
On the face of old Australia, hard and raw.
  Men from north of Boorooloola
  And as far south as Dimboola
And the western plains where sluggish rivers flow
  From unmeasured miles of mallee
  And the fertile Hunter Valley
Waiting patient by the chutes to have a go....
  To have a willing go....
  Riders part and parcel of the rodeo.

May the good Lord courage send us
For the Brahma bulls tremendous

Fiery eyes and stabbing horns and slashing tail
   Never mind the bumps and bruises
   They're the prizes for the losers
Make a bee-line for the bar dispensing ale.
   You will find it isn't funny
   If you're short on drinking money
But with luck you'll find a mate who has some dough
   It's a game for generous spending
   And a time for careless lending
If a bloke is dinky-di he won't say no....
   He won't say no....
   If you're part and parcel of the rodeo.

   There's some stag-meat barbecuing
   Bet your life it takes some chewing
Grab a steak and fill your tank, the day is long
   There'll be fun to follow later
   For both rider and spectator
When we finish after dark with wine and song.
   See the entertainment roster
   Terry Gordon and Stan Coster
At the dance to-night they're turning on a show
   So my lad put out a feeler
   You may win some sprightly sheila
There are lots of willing ones as well you know....
   As well you know....
   When you're part and parcel of the rodeo.

   When life's troubles sad attend you
   Some advice my friend I'll lend you
If misfortune's bitter wind begins to blow
   Let no woeful wowsers censure
   Take the pathway to adventure
Become part and parcel of the rodeo....
Part and parcel of the rodeo.

Ballad of Rabbiter Jim
(Or the life he knew only too well)

The bunnies were scarce, and old Rabbiter Jim
    was feeling the burden of years
He decided retirement was due now to him
    on a soft job that gave him no cares.
"I am weary", he said, "of the rabbits I seek,
    their fleas and their horrible smell
So I'll leave for the lights of the city next week,
    this life I know only too well".

"I'm tired of the frost and the cold wind that blows,
    The summer that brings burnin' heat
The wait-a-while bushes that tear at yer clothes
    and the gibbers that blister yer feet".
"I've eaten tough bunnies fried, roasted and boiled
    'til the taste nearly drives me insane
Too long in the bush for a pittance I've toiled,
    next week I'll be catchin' the train".

He left the black woman who cooked all his feeds
    every day in the galley and camp
And on cold nights took care of his natural needs
    after long weary hours on the tramp.
He left his bark humpy for better or worse,
    his horse and his old cattle dog
And he flung all his traps with an oath and a curse
    by the side of a stringbark log.

To the city of Sydney he journeyed afar,
    took a job at a pub in the 'Loo
With a bucket and mop, cleaning lounge-room and bar
    and the toilets where drunken bums spew.

But no friends could he find 'mid the tough Sydney push,
   and no peace, as my story will tell
And he missed his old cobbers outback in the bush
   and the life he knew only too well.

The foul city smog in his nose left a taint
   far worse than a rabbit's hot gore
And the publican drove him until he grew faint,
   demanding each day more and more.
He feared all the con-men and hoodlums that worked
   wicked crime undercover of dark
And the sinister ladies of evening who lurked
   in the laneways by alley and park.

The barmaids laughed long at his hard whiskery dial
   and the smell of the slops on his shoes.
The grim dockyard cops gave him no cause to smile,
   or the seamen who caused drunken blues.
The second-hand food that the guests overlooked
   was his share of the dinner each day
And he craved for the dampers his black woman cooked
   in the sandalwood scrub far away.

A need for old freedom he suddenly felt
   in mysterious bush wild and wide
With a bag for the bunnies tucked under his belt
   and his lantern and dog by his side.
"There's a train goes each week", he decided at last
   "so good-bye to this modernised hell
It's time I returned to the days of the past
   and the life I knew only too well".

So the bleary-eyed sinners who tipple and brag,
   with amusement were filled once again
At the bush pub, when Rabbiter Jim with his swag
   was seen to embark from the train.

He headed with speed to his old camping spot,
 quite ignoring the flies and the ants
And the thorns of the wait-a-while troubled him not
 as they grabbed at the seat of his pants.

The endless relief caused his hard soul to weep
 at the greeting expressed by his dog
Then with hopes of the future he grinned at the heap
 of traps by the stringybark log.
His faithful dark mistress was smoothing the cot
 she had just arrived back from the town,
And she raked from the ashes a fresh damper hot,
 with the crust cooked a deep shade of brown.

From a boiler the scent of roast bunny arose,
 and he happily chewed on a bone
While the rank smell of rabbit-blood tickled his nose
 like the odour of Eau de Cologne.
Now out in rough country where wages are slim,
 and the rich men are careful and tight
Moves the flickering lantern of Rabbiter Jim,
 like a will o' wisp in the night.

The sour smell of rabbit-blood clings to his clothes
 and his hands from the digging are rough
But he grins at the pelts drying out on the bows,
 for a living providing enough.
With his horse and his dog and his murri girl tall
 he explores every gully and dell
And freedom is his; though his profits are small
 it's a life he knows only too well.

The Wattlebenders

(In earlier days, the stockmen who performed the dangerous job of mustering wild cattle from the scrub country of southern Queensland, were known as "scrub dashers", "brush bashers", or more commonly, "wattlebenders". One of the few remaining to-day, is a mate of long standing, Duncan Marquard, of Goondiwindi....Author's note.)

The wattlebenders are gone, Duncan
   No more they ride to meet
The challenge of the big scrub bulls
   And yearlings fast and fleet
The wild old cows with horns like swords
   No more in thickets hide
The roaring tractors break the soil
   Where scrubland once was wide.
Mysterious, dark and lonely
   Holding its secrets well
Only the tales remaining
   That surviving old hands tell.

Where brigalow belts were dark and dense
   There now lies fallowed plain
The wattlebenders are gone, Duncan
   But a few like you remain
To tell how ringers brash and bold
   On horses lean and hard
Would run the wild scrub cattle out
   To many a branding yard
With lifted heads and upthrust tails
   And scared eyes rolling white
The buloke suckers crackling
   In the passage of their flight.

The game old stock-horse closing in
   Through dust-wrack rolling red

141

Like time's swift curtain shutting out
   An era past and dead
Do you think of the days you rode, Duncan
   Beside that reckless gang,
"Red Jack" and "Wattlebender" Smith
   "Green Hide" and "Ginger" Lang?
The horseback men of bygone times
   Who toiled from day to day
For the honour of their calling
   And a sadly niggard pay.

Hard were those hot pursuits, Duncan
   When saddles reeked with sweat
When clothing by dead boughs was torn
   And spurs with blood were wet.
Peaceful the sleep when night-winds played
   Amid the dark belars
Noisy the wild carousals held
   In lonely outback bars
Grey dawns and scarlet sunsets
   Rough meals of junk and tea
The never-ending scrubline green
   And endless as the sea.

No quarter asked or given then
   Hard lives in hardship wrought
Wild were the wattlebenders
   And wild the beast they sought.
When youthful hearts knew little fear
   Keen eyes no danger saw
But the long years have taken toll, Duncan
   And you'll dash through the scrub no more.
But perhaps your old mates are waiting
   Where the Jordan's waters are wide
And you'll meet with the wattlebenders
   When you get to the Other Side.

The Wide Horizon

The old adventurers hardy
  From ancient countries sailed
Where life was slow and tardy
  And poverty prevailed.
Some from great pomp and peerage
  The bluest blood on earth
Some who had travelled steerage
  On life's grim tide since birth.
They sought a wide horizon
  On wild lands vast and lone
Great wealth they set their eyes on
  To gild a nation's throne.

Dull native shores forsaking
  With hope a flag unfurled
Fond hearts behind them breaking
  Ahead the distant world.
Where jungle rivers slow run
  They faced with resolute heart
The tomahawk and blow-gun
  The spear and poisoned dart.
Seeking a new star ever
  On skylines far away
The boundless Never-Never
  Rhodesia's veldt and vlei.

Grim snowfields in Alaska
  The blizzard's blinding gale
The foaming Athabasca
  The freezing Klondyke trail.
By coral strands spray-beaten
  Where ceaseless rolled the tide

And gulls and crabs had eaten
  The flesh of men who died
Through swamps aglow with fever;
  On deserts raw and red
Where gold, the cruel deceiver
  Was always just ahead.

Scorning the weak and feckless
  On roads to riches bent
With courage cool and reckless
  Devoid of fear they went
From city slum oppressive
  Quiet farm and country lane;
The British lads aggressive
  The swarthy men of Spain
The Dutchman and the German
  The French and Belgians strong
They brooked no prayer or sermon
  Where ocean leagues were long.

Few found bejewelled prize on
  Those vast untrammeled lands
False was the wide horizon
  Where red gods gave commands.
Far on the frontiers scattered
  Living from day to day
Small lives that little mattered
  But still they blazed the way
For those that followed after
  The wealth to seize and hold
The rich man and the grafter
  Whose greed secured the gold.

Dull is the world around us
  We apathetic grow
A sheltered life has bound us
  On boring paths we go.

We suffer no privations
　Selfish and small our creeds
No more we conquer nations
　With daring hearts and deeds.
No wild red gods bedizen
　As old we grow and grey
There gleams no wide horizon
　To lure us forth to-day.

The Price of a Pearl

Broome, where the pearls are priceless,
  sinkhole of crime and sin
Where the human parasites gather
  when the luggers come sailing in.
There in the glow of the tropics
  the flotsam of many lands
Drifts on the tide of adventure
  to Capricorn's coral strands.

So a pearler anchored at sunset
  when the variant tide was low
And her English skipper was legend,
  the man known as Brummagem Joe
Gambler, brawler and drunkard,
  consort of criminals and whores
Cast in disgrace from his homeland
  to sail on exotic shores.

Priceless the pearl he had taken,
  quickly hidden from view
For he trusted no single member
  of his rag-tag, cut-throat crew.
Safe in his money-belt planted
  he treasured his find full well
A gift for the tall white harlot
  from Noumea, who was called Farelle.

Toast of the lugger captains,
  reaping a harvest of vice
Queen of the waterfront deadfalls,
  tarnished jewel for a price.
But two knew the pearl's existence
  and their hunger for riches grew

Kamoko Yasaki the tender,
and the shell-opener, Johnny Koru.

Men without conscience or scruple,
handy with sandbag and knife
The pearl in its value was greater
than any human life.
Out where the palm-fronds rustled,
heedless of God or the law
They watched that night in the darkness
by the lamplit house of the whore.

'Til came forth the English captain
and with steps unsteady he lurched
Soft was the thud of the sandbag
But in vain the vultures searched.
For no pearl there was for the taking
and they woke to a fact full well.
The bauble they sought so madly
was now in the hands of Farelle.

Consigned to the sea near a mangrove
was the body of Brummagem Joe
Where the gulls and landcrabs waited to feast
and a tiger-shark circled slow.
Drunk was the woman on wine and wealth
as she studied the captain's find,
Unaware of the greedy eyes that watched
through the slats in the bamboo blind.

Then hinges creaked and the door swung wide
announcing the murderous pair,
She knew in a flash that the pearl they sought
and displaying no panic or fear
She raised a hand to her open mouth
then followed it, swift as light

147

With a draught of wine from the brimming glass
  that shone like a ruby bright.
  At once Kasaka the tender guessed
  the gem's safe hiding place,
He spoke a command to his partner in crime
  with a terrible leer on his face.
And Johnny Koru was a shell-opener
  skilled at a nauseous trade,
Swift he reached for the knife at his belt,
  swift was the stroke he made.

He grinned at the twitching human shell
  where the pearl was, no need to ask,
With a murderous light in his slitted eyes
  he stooped to his grisly task.
'Til at length the guts of the butchered corpse
  its secret of wealth revealed
Then the shell-opener died by Kasaka's knife
  as in mucous and blood he kneeled.

The tender smiled at the bloodied pearl
  and thought of the joys in store
Then his dream fell dead as a police patrol
  came in through the open door.
Aware that the gallows awaited him now
  and the seeds of his fate were sown
He flung the pearl where the waters lapped
  and the ocean reclaimed its own.

Gone on the tide to the sea once more
  where the porpoises dive and play
And the octopus spread his curtain of ink
  to blind his unwary prey.
Gone from the greedy desires of man
  to the depth of the salty swirl;
Lover of fashionable jewels take heed
  Four lives was the price of the pearl.

148

Ballad of "Bugwine" Green

Come sit down and listen you shearer men
who gather to guzzle a beer
   I'll tell of a man who distilled heavy grog
   from the juice of the prickly pear.
On the potent product wild sprees were held
and his drinking mates never knew
   That the lifeblood of cacto-blastis bugs
   went into the ghastly brew.

A good supply was always maintained
in bottles and kegs unclean
   And held in highest esteem was the drink
   manufactured by Bugwine Green.
In a humpy he lived with a sad yellow girl
who he showed no kindness or care
   For his one true love was the bug-flavoured booze
   that he made from the prickly pear.

Now Bugwine's woman a hard time had
tormented both day and night
   By the drunken dead-beats who hung around
   from dawn til the stars were bright.
Something has to be done, she thought
Before all my hair turns grey
   I have to get rid of this drunken sot
   And there isn't an easy way.

But I'll patient be and wait me chance
and perhaps the hour will come
   When the Lord above will show me how
   to dispose of a worthless bum.

149

So the brewer's mates departed at last
to a shearing-shed far away
    And Bugwine fermented the cactus plants
    like a madman day after day.

He guzzled the brew and no tucker he bought
while his downtrodden wife grew lean
    And more powerful and potent every hour
    was the product of Bugwine Green.
A fifty-gallon barrel he filled
till it wouldn't hold any more
    Then down in a drunken torpor he sank
    on the liquor-stained kitchen floor.

Here is the chance, and it's time to act
the destitute woman thought
    While ever this tosspot is part of my life
    the future holds for me naught.
I'll rectify now the sorry mistake
of a wedding that shouldn't have been
    And she put into motion the dastardly plan
    that would rid her of Bugwine Green.

Two months went by, and the shearer men
returned full of joy one day
    They found no trace of brewer or wife
    and the hut was in sorry decay.
But firm stood the fifty-gallon keg
with the spigot driven tight
    "Our cobber has left us a drink", one said
    "and sample it well we might."

Like thirsty cattle they drank and drank
the spree lasted several days
    And the cactus brew had a meaty taste
    that earned much comment and praise.
"Wonder where Bugwine is", one said
"he's missin' an awful good drink"

150

But when they knocked in the head of the keg
what they found made each stomach shrink.

Their eyeballs rolled and their livers swelled
and their hair and beards turned grey
  And perhaps the ghoulish laughter they heard
  of a woman now far away.
Some of them took epileptic fits
while some sought to vomit and spew
  When the cause of the meaty taste they found
  in the dregs of the cactus brew.

For the withered horror that met their eyes
was a sight no man should have seen
  Curled in the keg and pickled like pork
  was the carcase of Bugwine Green.

Passing of Paddy

(A Queensland Legend)

Paddy Mulligan died from grog
　　On the road to Charleville
His corpse was found by a drover's dog
And his spirit sits on a coolibah log
When nights are hot and still
　　And it sings while ferocious fantods leer
　　"Carry me back to ould Kildare
　　There's plenty of Irish Whiskey there
　　And begorrah I'll have me fill".

Paddy was old and seamed and scarred
　　Fond of whiskey and Guinness' Stout
Fellers all paid him no regard
So he lived and laboured and perished hard
And at night you could hear his spirit shout
　　Loud, as the jim-jams danced with glee
　　"Carry me over the Irish Sea
　　There's plenty of grog for you and me
　　And 'twil cure me aches no doubt".

So we parcelled his bones and sent 'em away
　　To the hills of County Kerry
In the small green land where goblins play
And his spirit followed, the ringers say
And his relatives all made merry.
And at night the spirit's ghostly shoes
Make phantom tracks in the bogland' ooze
Crying "show me a place where there's lots of booze
　　And I'll take ye to Londonderry".

NEIL PERCIVAL

Duncan's Mate

In watercourses wet and grim
   Old Duncan lives in style
And should you chance to visit him
   He always wears a smile
And in the camp-fire's smokey haze
   Strange tales he will relate
Of mates he knew in early days
   From Gore to Poison Gate.
The ringers rough who rode and camped
   In seasons gone before
The soldier coves with whom he tramped
   To meet the dogs of war.

A rugged breed departed long
   From western hills and plains
Replaced by men not quite as strong
   But Duncan still remains.
To tell the yarns of joy and tears
   When mates were true and willing
The shameful sad depression years
   The fight to earn a shilling.
And still at times misfortune reigns
   But Duncan's not a loser
Of friends, as long as he maintains
   A mate as true as Boozer.

He lives content at Duncan's side
   And after years together
In long retirement they abide
   Through fair or stormy weather.
He's big and ugly, black and hard
   And awkward seems in motion

But holds for Duncan high regard
  That borders on devotion.
Self-sacrifice surpassing love
  All forms of doubt repelling
Consistent as the stars above
  His faith requires no telling.

And if for liquor Duncan yearns
  And goes his thirst a-sating
He's sure to find when he returns
  Old Boozer faithful waiting.
He doesn't care to have a spree
  But waits forlorn and lonely
His stock in trade is loyalty
  And love for one man only.
Determined, trusty, strong and stout
  As any battle cruiser
Pull out the flask!! I'll call a shout
  For Duncan's cobber Boozer.

We meet while travelling life's hard track
  Companions strange and varied
Some wise and kind, some mean and drack
  Some by misfortune wearied.
Old boyhood mates who understand
  Their passing sad bereaves you
The generous blokes with helping hand
  The girls who love and leave you.
The wealthy coves, the poor ones too
  The larrikin and bruiser
But you'll never meet a mate as true
  As Duncan's old dog Boozer.

NEIL PERCIVAL

Ballad of
Burdekin Bert

Burdekin Bert had humped his drum
  From Cairns to the Birdsville track
Fond he was of Bundaberg rum
  Strong and sticky and black.
Rung the board in a Warrego shed
  Then tramped to a town nearby
Where me met a sheila with tresses red
  And a coveteous gleam in her eye.

She won his heart, she was curvey and soft
  As my reader doubtless thinks
But she hated the booze and told him oft
  "I will marry no man who drinks".
And his shed-mates frowned and shook their heads
  At the woman's possessive stare
And one remarked, "If this tart he weds
  The trousers she'll always wear".

So he took the pledge and the drink he spurned
  At his lady-love's harsh behest
And with eyes on the future his steps he turned
  To the sheds in the distant west.
Where he ducked his head and tightened his belt
  And for six long months he shore
And though oft the desire for drink he felt
  He tackled the rum no more.

The last fleece fell, the last bell rang
  And sober as man could be
He turned aside from the drunken gang
  Who were bent on a perilous spree.
His intentions were honourable there is no doubt
  As he wearily hoisted his drum

But he longed for the pub and a long willing bout
　　With a bottle of Bundaberg rum.

He returned once again to the Warrego town
　　Where his lover had chosen to wait
And a date for the wedding was quickly set down
　　As the summery season grew late.
So up to the altar in step with his bride
　　In tails and a bullet-proof shirt
A responsible man with a strong steady pride
　　Walked the shearer called Burdekin Bert.

"A beautiful couple", the onlookers said
　　As they dignified walked down the aisle
And the gentle old parson with snowy white head
　　Gave the lovers a warm friendly smile.
"Do you take this woman faithful and true?"
　　And the bride smirked possessively
Then the bridegroom knew if he said "I do"
　　His soul would never be free.

And he saw himself tied for the rest of his life
　　By petticoat government curtailed
And his cash would be grabbed by a dominant wife
　　And his ears by a harsh tongue assailed.
"I do NOT", he yelled and his voice woke the dead
　　And the crowd of well-wishers stood dumb
Save an old mate who dropped in his hand as he fled
　　A bottle of Bundaberg rum.

So again for the shearer the old life began
　　A wild rebel no marriage could tame
And the bride soon recovered and married a man
　　Who a downtrodden doormat became,
So I ask you my readers which end is the worst
　　In this dull world of struggle and strife
To be an old bum by the bottle accursed
　　Or a slave for a dominant wife?

158

The Beastly Brahma

Ho! I've been a wild ringer in seasons gone by
   And all breeds of cattle at times I have mustered
And the term "safe and gentle" will never apply
   For there isn't a bovine on earth to be trusted.
But the biggest headache for the cattle-farmer
Is the horrible brute they call the Brahma.

The Santa Gertrudis is a Spanish innovation
   That drives the stockman right out of his senses
The piebald Friesian, a dairying sensation
   Is extremely capable at knocking down fences.
But humped like a camel and sour as a llama
There's no beast as bad as the big ugly Brahma.

The Shorthorn is noted for size and docility
   And at beef exhibitions defeats every rival
But in dry times displays no capability
   At resisting the drought and sustaining survival
A species placid, with temper calmer
He differs from the odiferous Brahma.

The Jersey and Guernsey are prone to mastitis
   The Ayrshire a mask like a robber displays
The red Illawarras with bellows afright us
   And soon lose condition if not on good graze.
But strap on a sword and a stout suit of armour
Before you approach the detestable Brahma.

The Hereford is susceptible to blight
   Because his white face lacks all pigmentation
The black Poll Angus stampedes in great fright
   And drives the drover to intoxication
But order a coffin and ring the embalmer
Before you go near the unlovable Brahma.

NEIL PERCIVAL

L'Envoi
(To the Ringers)

Western sunset; the night birds are flying
    As the days of our lives flit away
In our dotage; no hope of denying
    The powers that reduce us to clay.
The leggings hang twisted and cracking
    The girth-straps are perished and old
The sad boots for polish are lacking
    And the saddle lies garnished with mould.

And I think when at times reminiscing
    (A painful procedure at best)
Of the faces and voices now missing
    By the passage of years laid to rest.
Old mates of the headrope and bridle
    Where success was a hope that was small
Always willing and strong, never idle
    Caring not should they rise or they fall.

With no mordant ambition expounding
    Welded hard in privation's grim mould
Standing strong 'til the last trump was sounding
    Undesiring of status or gold.
Old mates, will you wait my arrival
    From the wide land where careless we rode
When the watchwords were faith and survival
    On the plains where the big rivers flowed.

Will you bear me a loud boisterous greeting
    On the heavenly stock-camps afar
Will we drink and carouse at the meeting
    As we once did in shanty and bar,
Will the stockwhips again be resounding
    When the blood on the spurs glistens red

And in darkness when wild hooves are pounding
As the thunderbolts flash overhead.

Will we welcome each bleary-eyed camper
Matter not who or what he may be
"Boil the can! spread the corn junk and damper
Here's a hungry bloke landed for tea".
Will the lost loves forever come stealing
Firing old lusts extinguished before
When we dallied while white stars were wheeling
Building dreams of a future once more.

Vanished life by old memories attended
Hang the bridle and spurs on the wall
For the day of the ringer is ended
And the old hands await final call
To a judgement unproved and uncertain
That I face with a tired heavy heart
Close the casket, draw slowly the curtain
As the sons of the saddle depart.

Verses of a Vagrant

Keith Garvey

Foreward

Not surprisingly, the two world wars of 1914-18 and 1939-45 and their aftermaths brought profound changes in the nature of Australia and its people.

During the decades of growth and discovery immediately before and after the turn of the century our national character, in both its reality and its mythology, was being forged. Its basis was mainly in the bush, and its progress was both mirrored and modified in moulding by the writers of the time.

The widening of our experience during the first global war, the upheavals, Gallipoli, then the homecoming to brief boom times and later depression, while in many ways implanting Australia's legends more firmly, widened the gap between myth and reality for most of her people. And the even more radical changes flowing from World War 2, the drift to the cities, the affluent society, mass immigration and technological advance have destroyed much, though of course not all, of the old ways.

All these years later we scarcely would have believed that anything of importance could be added to the wonderful picture that Lawson, Paterson, Furphy, Steele Rudd, Ogilvie and the rest of the writers for the old Bulletin, writing with such lusty national pride of "young Australia growing like a weed", had left for us. They had said it all, we believed, for their generations.

Keith Garvey has proved us wrong.

Born four years after WW 1 ended, Garvey was five months old when Lawson died. But he grew up in a place and time when, though the old Australia was already fading into history, its echoes were still ringing strongly in the memories of the old-timers, in the folk yarns that abounded in the bush, and indeed in the lifestyles and habits of the common people in Garvey's country, around the Gwydir and the Mehi and westward to the arid interior.

Lacking a formal education, Keith spent a lifetime as a peer of the humblest orders of the bush workers — the shearers, the drovers, the ringers and fencers and dingo shooters — the people who were the last to receive the changes and the sometimes doubtful benefits of "progress". They were the living residue of the "real Australians", and in every sense, Keith was one of them. His contact with the vanishing past may have been delayed, but it was no less real for that. When he wishes, Keith can write with keen perception of today's world too, but it is the echo of yesterday's Australia that he evokes for us most eloquently.

All the bush writers of the Bulletin were men familiar with the bush, Lawson particularly having spent his formative years as close as one could get to the earth with which his writing was to be concerned. But Garvey is unique in that he spent a lifetime knowing nothing else: when he began to write, ten years ago, he was older than Lawson was when the Old Master died.

Garvey's work is the product of a fertile imagination and a fluent command of language, editing and refining a fund of lore collected at its source over a lifetime. He distils from these elements the very spirit of the people who made Australia, the soul of that once heartbreakingly hard country west of the coastal ranges. And beyond that there is a universal element which gives us an insight into all men who have struggled all through history, and into our own times and ourselves.

And the real importance of his work is that it doesn't simply re-state Paterson and Lawson. From a more detached time platform Keith Garvey can and does show us a new dimension. Among the chroniclers who give us an understanding of one of the key periods in the making of Australia, the self-styled "scribe from the scrub" must in time come to rank with the rest of the giants.

Eric Watson

168

Dedication
to Laura
(Brief romance, painful parting)

These are the verses the vagrants write
  By cattle-camp, hut and tent
In the gloomy dark of silent night
  When memory strikes like ghoulish blight
With regret for the days misspent.

Oh, the rebel path has remote reward.
  We follow, no gold to glean
Addressing no man as sir or lord
Wasters by parson and priest deplored
  Disbarred from the social scene.

Setting our steps on freedom's road
  Laws a depressing bain
Seeking no comfort or safe abode
Grinding the seed that Red Gods sowed
  Wandering the wastes like Cain.

And I wonder oft, if in days to come
  Where ever you now might be
Red-haired girl from the Dublin slum
Whose soul to the voice of love was dumb
  Will you remember me?

Vagrant's Dwelling

A stubborn bloke who won't conform
   My rebel ways are flagrant
I've followed long through strife and storm
   The pathways of the vagrant.
There's times I've often cursed the swag
   When heavy it was growin'
In sands that cause yer feet to lag
   On western deserts glowin'.

Yer brains yer reckon must be fried
   And yer bones for rest are cryin'
And yer swear yer'll chuck the load aside
   Walk on and leave it lyin'.
Just like the load of want and wear
   And doubts and fears that fetter
But yer know you've got too old to care
   Or try for something better.

Great youthful hopes no longer come
   Old dreams the long years sever.
And yer curse the day yer slung the drum
   And wish it gone forever.
When sorrerful regret hard rides
   On conscience far from placid
And the seat is threadbare in yer strides
And the tucker-bag is flaccid.

I've humped the drum for gain or loss
   Tired, destitute and ragged
As to Golgotha with the cross
   Our Saviour bravely staggered.
But when at dark cold shadows creep
   And aches and pains bereave me
I roll her out and fall asleep
   The swag is home, believe me.

White Cliffs

Heaps of shale red white and brown
  Baking 'neath the burnished sky
Heat waves caper up and down
On the little mining town
  White cliffs, where the opals lie.
Crippled and misshapen land
  By the hand of Nature maimed
Temperature a fiery brand
Waterless the smouldering sand
  By the imps of Hell proclaimed.
Still a frontier outpost lone
  Craggy rampart, dusty ditch
Everlasting rock and stone
Where the seeds of wealth are sown
  For the one who strikes it rich
Sad acasias silent droop
  Like the drooping dreams of men
Who saw wealth in one swift swoop
Still in shafts they hopeful stoop
  Always wondering 'if' and 'when'.

Hearts to hardship long innured
  Much to gain and naught to lose.
Heat and hunger cruel endured
Hope they oft can scarce afford
  Activated by the booze.
Night falls soft with furtive stealth
  Still there glitters one bright star
Weary bodies, broken health
Still you hold their dream of wealth
  White cliffs, where the opals are.

171

To The True Stockmen

(The Stockmens Hall of Fame at Longreach, Qld will be officially opened by Her Majesty the Queen on April 29...News Item)

(The following verses are dedicated to the true stockmen of Australia, and particularly my old mate Duncan Marquard, a ringer without peer, long retired).

Her Majesty is coming out, a Queen
   who wins acclaim
And she's going up to Longreach to
   the Stockmens Hall of Fame
To open it officially, an honour, I
   declare
You can bet the wealthy moguls and
   their ladies will be there
At this grand and gilded building, it's
   erected so they say
In fond memory of the stockmen that
   we knew in earlier day.
There'll be lots of cosy bureaucrats
   in costly city wear
Folk who wouldn't know a stock-horse
   from a drought-struck Brahma steer.
Never had to fork a rough one,
   sitting out the bumps and jars,
Riding only plush upholstery
   in their air-conditioned cars.
They will offer flowery speeches
   when the champagne starts to fizz
They will toast the men with millions,
   and our Sovereign Lady Liz.

They'll congratulate each other, drink
   and feast 'till all is blue

172

But it's time I reckon Duncan
　　that they honoured men like you.
The true Australian stockmen,
　　men whose deeds remain untold,
By the absentees exploited
　　in the days when beef was gold.
Battling hard to make a living
　　in a raw unconquered land
While the wool-kings back in England
　　watched their bank accounts expand.

Lonely men who did the hard part, with
　　the red dirt for a bed
When the pay was just a pittance, scarce
　　enough to keep them fed.
When the sleety rain seemed endless
　　and the blankets always damp
And a bad horse tried to get you every
　　morning on the camp.
Ration tea and mouldy damper, salt meat
　　with a sewer-pipe smell
From a summer sun that blasted like a
　　welding torch in Hell.
Curry far too oft reheated in a black
　　Bedouri pot
Dysentry that drained the system,
　　prickly heat and Barcoo rot.
Drinking water brack and tainted, often
　　ravish for a smoke.
Swilling plonk at wayside shanties
　　saddling up again dead broke.
Watching fat men growing fatter
　　while all hope of fortune flew
Little doubt about it, Duncan
　　we should honour men like you.

Daring dashes through the brigalow
　　when the breakaways took flight

173

Watches long when nerves wore ragged
  as the storm clouds rolled at night.
Desperate moments on the dogwatch
  as the thunder boomed and growled
And the wild mob rose unsettled
  every time a dingo howled.
Lightning flashing wild at midnight
  when the cattle rushed in fear
And the long horns gleamed like sabres
  in the blue electric glare.
Dirty blanket for a coffin when a
  ringer's horse went down
Shallow grave without a marker on
  the sandhill's lonely crown.
Godless men by Gods unheeded
  with all faith and creed destroyed
In a bitter feudal system by the
  bloated rich employed.
Not for them cigars and whiskey like
  the wealthy social crew,
It is not surprising, Duncan
  that we honour men like you.

Men who won no decorations
  but who saw the job was done
Pushed aside by automation on each
  distant Northern run.
Lonely nights by smokey camp-fires,
  thoughts of old home far away
And for some a woman waiting, ever
  faithful day by day.
Not for them the golden handshake that
  our statesmen fat receive,
Potter's Field and pauper's casket,
  very few to mourn or grieve
And the Hall of Fame is something that
  is sadly overdue
To commemorate the stockmen Duncan,
  ringers tough like you.

174

Red Rock

White with foam the breakers tumbling
On the carmined buttress crumbling
  Where the river meets the sea
Overhead the white gulls screaming
As the setting sun is beaming
  Red as blood on Calvary.

Soft the paperbark trees rustle
Far from wearing din and bustle
  Where the city beacons glow
Sandy hillocks downward sweeping
Silent vigil ever keeping
  Over ebb and tide below.

Loud the mighty coamers thundering
Set my restless spirit wondering
  What we profit at the last
Puny man the gods defying
Heeding not the short years flying
  Sees not Nature's bounty vast.

Little sand-beach spread before me
You have never ceased to draw me
  With your spell of savage peace
With your solitude enraptured
Will my soul by you be captured
  Red Rock, when my heartbeats cease?

Memories of School

The town of Pallamallawa sits silently at rest
   As years go by it neither blooms or fades
It isn't quite like other towns, the citizens attest
   Oft the scene of wild and lawless escapades.
It was there I spent my boyhood,
   gained an education short
   At the little school surviving still today
We gave lessons small attention,
   but found lots of time for sport
   Making room for ceaseless mischief on the way.

Then no transport was available the pupils to convey
   We walked or rode an old decrepit steed
And our lack of simple knowledge
   drove the patient teacher grey
   Brilliant scribes or scholars there were few indeed.
Teacher's insight keen was lacking,
   but his discipline was not
   Child psychology was imparted with the cane
And oft in fear and trembling we sat rooted to the spot
   While the sinners howled regretfully with pain.

Laymen countless were produced,
   but no barristers-at-law
   No genius gaining everlasting fame
Save a bullock driver's son by the name
   of Ken McCaw
   And the State Attorney General he became.
   Words of great Imperial writers, Wordsworth, Kipling,
Keats and Scott
Were propounded to us time and time again
But the works of Henry Lawson most decidedly were not
   Lest a Socialistic outlook we attain.

There is modern transport now,
  where on bush tracks long ago
  In depression days the barefoot children tramped
The old classmates that I knew to the mists of memory go
  And a sporting complex stands where swagmen camped.
But if I could shed the years,
  turn the hands of time once more
  Back to boyhood where the Gwydir wends it's way
I'd relive the education I neglected long before
  At the old bush school still standing strong today.

The Abominable Rat

A devil incarnate I creep through the night
   Hated renegade banished like Cain
In the garbage-can's contents I find great delight
   And the alley cat seeks me in vain.
From soiled rags and rubbish a nest I construct
   In hovels and sewers dark and deep
And for food stale and mouldy a search I conduct
   While the householders heavily sleep.
With fangs hard as chisels swifty entry I make
   In ceilings and cupboards as well
I defile meat and bread, I destroy cheese and cake
   Sharp my claws and offensive my smell.

With poisons and traps I am constantly sought
   But for centuries long I have thrived
For with Man the oppressor my species has fought
   Since the dawning when Adam arrived.
   With great skills and cunning a feast I would seize
   At the banquets when Nero was great
And I ate bloated bodies and spread foul disease
   In the carnage that all wars create.
The Black Plague's fine microbes I sought to appease
   When through London they swept like a tide
For I was the landlord who hosted the fleas
   That spread famine and death far and wide.

From the dank dreary hideouts the dockyards provide
   I come searching suspicious and sly
In the holds of the vessels that rock on the tide
   Swift destroyer of cargoes am I.
The castles of monarchs provide me a home
   And the labourer's humble abode
And oft to the fields of the farmer I roam
   Sampling crops he conveniently sowed.
In all lands on earth I grow prosperous and fat
   And in millions my coherts attend
Let weak Man tread softly for I AM KING RAT
   A scourge 'til the world meets its end.

The Shearin's on Again

Put a crimp in bluey boys, the shearin's on again
  The musterers are saddlin' up on every hill and plain
See the kelpies workin' wide where the big mobs spread
Pushin' up the laggard tail or castin' far ahead.
The cook is in the kitchen, stokin' up the coals
  Mincin' stringy stag-meat for curries and rissoles.
Time to leave the Cross behind, gaudy girls and beer
  Roll yer swag and scarper, the shearin' time is here.

Put a crimp in bluey boys, the shearin's on again
  Holidays are over now, it's time to catch the train
Get the combs and cutters out, clean away the rust
  Western sheds are kickin' off, it's back a' Bourke or bust.
That's the place where every day the big guns cut the deuce.
Land where men are mostly men and laws are
  fast and loose.
Let's go where the rouseabouts pray all night for rain
  Westward where the brolgas dance,
  the shearin's on again.

Put a crimp in bluey boys, there's money to be had
  Cash for willin' workers and battlers goin' bad
Mulga wethers big and rough, hard merino ewes
  Providin' pain and backache for fellers on the booze.
Dainty little hoggets good for fifty every run
Encouragin' the learner who desires to be a gun.
Tighten up your dungarees, show a willin' heart
  Hop in boys and get a quid, the shearin's due to start.

Put a crimp in bluey boys, the shearin's on again
  Dry and sunny weather makes the rouseabouts complain
Ninety bucks a hundred now, hear the squatters squawk
  Fraser's in the discard, here's success to Mr Hawke.
See the ringer knuckle down, he's a hungry cow
  Streams of sweat and brilliantine pourin' down his brow.
Stokin' up on aspirin and rum to ease the strain
  Duck yer heads and graft boys, the shearin's on again.

179

Middle Cut O' Brisket
(A Duffer's Delight)

Beef today for dinner
    Onion sauce and spuds
Strewth she looks a winner
    'Light and dust yer duds.
Hungry riders waitin'
    To enjoy the feast
Middle cut o' brisket
    Best cut on the beast.
Bellies small and shrunken
    Soon will fill once more
Get the bottle, Duncan
    London Bob can pour.

Middle cut o' brisket
    Salted boiled and strained
Middle cut o' brisket
    Illegally obtained.

Sick of eatin' tomcats
    Snake and kangaroo
Brumby goats and wombats
    Break yer heart to chew.
Hard we rode by starlight
    To a neighbourin' run
Back before the far light
    Heralded the sun.
Packbags full and leakin'
    Salt and bloodied brine
See the old cook seekin'
    Slices fat and fine.

Middle cut o' brisket
    Steamin' in the pot

Middle cut o' brisket
  Eat it cold or hot.

Chew the tasty tallow
  Piled up on the plate
Ringers shrewd or callow
  All declare it great
Have another helpin'
  Never fear the traps
Hear the heelers yelpin'
  Hungry for the scraps.
Johnny cake and damper
  Soakin' up the grease
See how every camper
  Eats in joy and peace.

Middle cut o' brisket
  Temptin' every thief
Middle cut o' brisket
  Finest cut o' beef.

("My oath, mate!")

Advice to a Young Friend

Gingerbread girl with the winning smile
   How many hearts will you beguile?
When will you find a lover to wed?
   Who do you dream of, Gingerbread?

Will he be handsome, dark and strong
   Or a hippy type with hair grown long?
Or a gambling man with a fortune won
   Or a country cove from an outback run?
Marry for money or fond love true
   Gingerbread girl, which will you do?

Days of our youth are quickly sped
   Make the most of them, Gingerbread.
Waste no time on sorrow or tears
   All too short are the fleeting years.
Old and worn we depart from the scene
   Mourning for what we might have been.

Sagging tummies and greying hair
   Burdened with conscience hard to bear.
Crippled and crotchety, short of breath
   Weary of life and afraid of death.
Fearing the sound of the Reaper's tread.
   Live for the moment, Gingerbread!

To A Top Rider

Well I recall my youthful days
   And the ringers who ride no more
Seldom now is a horseman seen
   Gone from the rolling pastures green
     Where the tractors grind and roar.
Life grows dull as the big machines
   Break the soil where the brigalows grew
   Men of the saddle are fled for aye
   By mechanised progress swept away
     Lost is the life I knew.

How do you find it, Johnny Roberts?
   Reaping the storm the wind has sown
   Feeling the pressure of passing years
   And the scars of fate a wild life wears —
     Now your fame with the years has flown.
Remember the good times, Johnny Roberts
   Top in the rodeo's garish flair
   Before you sought an easier life
   Far from the show-ring's strain and strife
     Feeling the worse for wear.

Waiting your turn at the chute unfearing
   Sweat on the shoulders, nostrils wide
   On a feature horse that showmen claim
   Is king of the ring in a risky game
     A bucker no man can ride.
Yours was a hard school, Johnny Roberts
   Mustering camps where the toil was tough
   Where the riding stock were a brumby mob
   If you didn't stay on you lost your job
     And the pay was never enough.

Holding your own with the best of riders
Drinking of gaudy fame your fill
Champion brash by the fans adored
Spurring high with a bold accord
And a cool and reckless skill.
Swift fly the short years, Johnny Roberts
Taking their toll with no mercy shown
Memories are all that now remain
Since you tackled the best for a paltry gain
For your fame with the years has flown.

Neglected Heroes

I took a trip to Charing Cross on a
  wintry day and raw
Lord Nelson's statue stands there,
  and regretfully I saw
How high and cold his column is,
  and sad it was to note
That England's naval hero bold wore
  no warm overcoat.

But resolute and firm he was as when
  wounded sore he lay
On the Victory's shattered quarter-deck
  at grim Trafalgar Bay.
'Twas a sad and careless oversight by
  every British peer
To leave Lord Nelson in the rain
  with no overcoat to wear.

And in the bar that afternoon
  I thought with deep regret
Of all the unsung heroes who go coatless
  in the wet
Who when wounded by misfortune
  never wilt or cry enough
Life the hero of Trafalgar when
  the odds he faced were tough.

Men who fight a willing battle
  but who never reach the top
In their dotage sadly lacking for
  a place to eat and flop.
And our statesmen fat and placid
  ought to spend a little more
On constructing homes and shelters
  for the ancient and the poor.

Depression Days

They were driven out by poverty from every city area
   A beaten disillusioned unconsidered human tide
That spilled unchecked across Australia's
   limitless interior
   Victims of a failing system, by society cast aside
Disregarded willing workers seeking labour non-existent
   In a land of full and plenty owned by combines far away
People sullen and resentful as their future hopes
   grew distant
      Muttering grimly of rebellion, swearing oft
         to have their day.

Homeless transient men and women by the
   rich and fat derided
      Building humpies in the timber from adjacent
         bark and pole
Pitching tents along the river where
   the rabbits food provided
      Knowing cruel humiliation when they went
         to draw the dole.
Then a maniac in Europe caused a bloody conflagration
   And soon afterwards the people suffered
      woe and want no more
For unending was the bounty that attended
   every nation
      An economy reconstructed through
      a sad and senseless war.

In the greatest land existing once again
   we face depression
      Will we see a repetition of our
         earlier bad mistakes?
Have the people gained the knowledge
   to combat today's recession

Can we rectify the wrongs before
   the restless war-god wakes?
Let us sacrifice our dull ideals to build
   a better future
   Cast aside our awful apathy and cease
      desultory talk
'Ere we feel the painful pressure of
   a foreign tyrant's Blucher
   Rally strongly little people,
      lead us boldly Mr Hawke!

The Chicken Hawk

Emitting loud his murderous squawk
  Round fowl-coops flits the Chicken Hawk
In sober plumage brown and buff
  He's very small, but very tough
Resembling not the famous Bob
  This little hawk is quite a snob
You never see him hanging round
  The trees where other birds abound
He loves instead the open sky
  Showing cruel beak and wicked eye
A loner whose sadistic looks
  Are terrifying to the chooks.

A killer bold since time began
  He gamely flouts the laws of man
And finally cops a shotgun blast
  Then dies a rebel to the last
For readers, it is plain to see
  He cannot bribe the powers that be
Unlike the crims who peddle drugs
  And coppers who shake down the mugs
The politicians full of guile
  Who con us with deceitful smile
And lots of other birds of prey
  Protected by the bribes they pay.

And so I think my rhyme explains
  The chicken hawk has got no brains.

Song Of The Bludger

In luxury and comfort I daily abide
    Waxing prosperous on sin-tarnished gains
Quite a sumptuous living my labourers provide
    By their work in dark alleys and lanes.
Like small children lost for protection they come
    And find themselves quickly enslaved
Then off to the cesspits in dockyard and slum
    To their calling both lewd and depraved.

Of social reformers and police I care naught
    Or the ranting of parson and priest
By a modest percentage the law is soon bought
    For together all vultures must feast.
And should thought of rebellion my workers acquire
    With great skill the razor I wield
And deeper they sink in the underworld's mire
    Their fate by disfigurement sealed.

So the sins of lost women provide my cigars
    Rich wines and expensive liqueurs
Loud suits and gold watches, plus new modern cars
    Hard won by the shame of the whores.
And when old and unlovely I cast them aside
    Fresh young talent forever abound
For incessant the flotsam drifts in on the tide
    And the hare will fall prey to the hounds.

So lazy and fat I continue to thrive
    Like a demon the foolish I seize
And with fear and misgiving the harlots must strive
    Their master and lord to appease.
'Til the day I am gripped by the Reaper's grim claws
    Then adieu to a world unrelentant
With a cortege composed of decrepit old whores
    To the grave I will go unrepentant.

Tripe

I always like a feed of tripe
   With onion sauce and peas
Black pepper and a dash of salt
   Then sprinkled well with cheese.
And when outback in early days
   A beast for meat was killed
The tripe was always well prepared
   By cooks renowned and skilled.
But in those hard and toilful times
   Of weariness and sweat
A bullock wasn't often killed
   So tripe was hard to get.

But lots of tripe there is today
   As you can plainly see
Supplied by maundering idiots
   Each evening on TV.
Our much respected media
   A special brand puts out
For unenlightened people
   To devour without a doubt.
And oft when regulations wear
   I long to take a swipe
At shallow bureaucrats who serve
   An endless feast of tripe.

The tripe religious groups dish out
   At times is hard to take
And promises are so much tripe
   That politicians make.
The tripe we get on radio
   Is hard to wear at best
And tripe that academics write

I simply can't digest.
And musical commercials
  Are a weird and dreadful type
Of food to feed illiterates
  May the fates destroy such tripe.

But blokes who moan can never win
  And I've complained enough
Let's dream of when the land was free
Although the track was rough.
So sharpen well the saw and knives
  And run the gantry up.
A straggler steer is in the yard
  Tonight like lords we sup
On steak and damper camp-fire cooked
  And pungent onions ripe
And for tomorrow well prepared
  A tasty feed of tripe.

The Carpenter's Message

Missiles of death that modern powers employ
  Relentless seeking greater wealth and spoil
With ruthless greed the skilful work destroy
  Of placid carpenters who patient toil
Waving no gory battle flag unfurled
  Seeking only with simple faith to give
Security to a sad and troubled world
  Where mankind in a tranquil peace might live.

Like one who chose the martyr's bitter path
  Dying in torment to redeem us all
And in his pain forgave the foolish wrath
  Of unenlightened fellow creatures small.
Shall we, when nuclear monsters rabid feed
  And callous ebbs and flows the crimson tide
Seek at the end his message old to heed
  The carpenter who was long ago denied.

The Chemist

In mediaeval times the drugs were made of
  ground-up bats
    Spittle drawn from toads and frogs
      and blood of snakes and rats
The old hands swore by herbalists who kill
  more than they save
    And rough bush medications were a quick
      way to the grave
Crude healers who believe in faith, and quacks
  who flout the laws
    The silly folk who rack their cues with
      brummy cancer cures.
The modern medications now most bad complaints
  have wrecked
    So here's luck to the chemist,
      a man we all respect.

The chemist is a friendly bloke reserved
  and quietly spoken
    He sells us bandages and splints for
      any limb that's broken.
Girdles right for matrons fat,
  that cause their sides to bust
    Rubber goods for teenage louts
      consumed by sinful lust.
Aspirin for headaches, mixtures for the 'flu
  Pills for sluggish kidneys that turn
    the urine blue.

Tasty toothpaste guaranteed to make
  the molars bright
    Lactogen for cranky kids who howl
      and scream all night.

Pills for constipated coves that make
  intestines glow
  Meds each month for dainty girls
    to halt their natural flow.
Hangover concoctions for the fellers on the spree
  Painful penicillin prods to counteract V.D.
Lotion for a skin disease, pads for corns that pain
  Morphia for lunatics to dull the maddened brain.

Gaudy labels to bewitch the ignorant
  and the poor
  Only psychological, they still effect
    a cure.
So if you have rheumatic pains or a gouty knee
  Drop in on the gentlemen at the pharmacy.
Trust him to produce a dope your illness
  to correct
  Here's luck to the chemist,
    a man you all respect.

Fraser vs Hawke
(Federal Election 1983)

Faced we many tough elections
  Since old Alfred Deakin ruled
Voters oft made bad selections
  Then discovered they were fooled.
Every Socialist well-wisher
  Loud the flowery praises sang
Of the men like Andy Fisher
  Chifley, Curtin and Jack Lang.

How the Tories hearts will gladden
  When they prate of better times
Menzies, Holt and Artie Fadden
  Win acclaim in prose and rhymes.
Now controversy unending
  Sweeps the city, bush and town
On electoral struggle pending
  For Australia's Federal crown.

Will the man whose public image
  Claims Australian hearts today
Conquer the forthcoming scrimmage
  Where the Liberals now hold sway?
Or will Tories taste the nectar
  Of another victory bold?
Tell me well, oh wise elector
  Who will win the fame and gold?

It's a pretty tricky question
  Who is wrong and who is right?
And the hustings make suggestion
  Of a hard and bitter fight

Ruthless statesmen seeking lustre
  Fruity policies extoll
Till the hour electors muster
  For the settling at the poll.

Grabbing golden tray and platter
  Plus a safe place in the sun
You can bet the muck will splatter
'Ere the Federal seats are won.
Fifth of March the day of reckoning
Action swift, no chance to baulk
Fame and fortune ceaseless beckoning
  When the Razor meets the Hawke.

Ballad Of A
Conscientious Australian

A blue-tongue sat drinking a pot of beer
  With a red kangaroo debating
He said, "The winter is drawing near
  It is time I was hibernating
I am off to a place called Wytaliba
  Far over New England ranges
To where the alternative lifestyles are
  And the climate never changes.
Where the dwellers live for delight and fun
  No effort or work employing
And they sit and loaf all day in the sun
  Their marihuana enjoying."

Said the kangaroo as he rolled a smoke
  "My friend, you many think me dippy
But I feel I am hardly the sort of bloke
  Who would make a successful hippy.
I couldn't reside in a grubby hut
  By the fumes of pot-weed strangled
With a swarm of lice in a beard uncut
  And long dirty hair entangled.
I could wear no ear-ring or metal chain
  Or other insane regalia
With a heritage proud I still remain
  A symbol of true Australia."

The One-Eyed Monster

When to school I used to go
Lots of things I didn't know
   Teacher grimly fought
To inject a bit of sense
In my skull so sadly dense
   Efforts came to naught.

Though I didn't care for school
Still I wasn't quite a fool
   I could read and write
In those earlier days we had
No TV to send us mad
   So I read at night

Shakespeare, Dickens, Kipling too
All their work I battled through
   Scott as well! Lord save me
Finding that no school or college
Could impart to me the knowledge
   That these masters gave me.

Now I am author noted
From the shearing sheds promoted
   And the cattle yard
Gained my education reading
No TV my mind impeding
   No more labour hard.

So kind parents of today
Heed the words I have to say
   Television's over-rated
Drag it to the river's brink
Heave it in and watch it sink
   Books make children educated.

The Sad Birds of Government

("A mysterious character known as The Goanna is
reported to be causing much friction between Mr
Hawke and Mr Peacock" .... News Item)

In the tall nest of Government where big birds
    are caged
    There was strife such as never before
Both the Hawke and the Peacock were greatly enraged
    And they ruffled their feathers for war.
"Friend Hawke" said the Peacock,
    "With truth I can say
    That as leader your efforts are lax
For you eat up the eggs that the little birds lay
    In the form of a new income tax.
The pigeons and gulls with great hunger grow thin
    While the vultures and crows feast at will
In the coming election you can't hope to win
    And my followers squawk for a kill."

Said the Hawke, "My friend Peacock,
    your words I gainsay
    You are quite misinformed, I can see
For the smart birds their nest-eggs have
    hidden away
    And to find them a hard job 'twill be.
These shrewd cunning birds are aware we are lost
    So their assets I feel I must freeze
For their valuable eggs would soon cover the cost
    Of our perilous flights overseas."
So the argument raged like a storm for a week
    While the lesser birds all bashed their lugs
Then down flew the Heron, a fish in his beak
    And said "Hey, pull together, you mugs."

"A sinister reptile is stalking you hard
　　He has been in the news every day
And for birds of importance he shows no regard
　　He advances intending to slay.
He is called the Goanna, true birds trust him not
　　Please forget your remarks so unkind
He will smile when he places you both in a spot
　　And the small birds new leaders will find.
Pull together and lead in a flight to success
　　'Ere our industry stops to a walk
And our wonderful country gets in a sad mess
　　Please co-operate, Peacock and Hawke.''

The Bushland Election
(March 5, 1983)

All the bush creatures clapped and cheered
When the gallant Liberal statesmen appeared
  But the mopoke croaked "bobork! bobork!"
The kookaburra led a grand ovation
The kangaroo yelled "They're the strength
  of the nation
A party that saves us from degradation"
  But the mopoke croaked "bobork! bobork!"

"Who will help us?" cried the dingo pup
"When the Franklin River is all dammed up?"
  And the mopoke croaked "bobork! bobork!"
"We all must stick with Treasurer Howard"
Said the crow, "Or the banks will be overpowered
The Whitlam Government our hearts has soured".
  So the mopoke croaked "bobork! bobork!"

The platypus rose from the gloomy water
And said "Vote for Mal I think we orter"
  But the mopoke croaked "bobork! BOBORK!!!"
"I'm drawing the dole" said the native cat
"I'm sure the Liberals won't alter that"
"They will get my vote" said the kangaroo rat
  But the mopoke screeched "bobork! bobork!"

When votes were counted on Sunday morn
All the animals looked forlorn
  And the mopoke leered "bobork! bobork!!"
They hoped for a Liberal Government respected
And wept when they heard who had been elected
So they hied themselves off feeling sad and dejected
  While the mopoke sneered "bobork!! BOBORK!!!"

The Fatal Stew

The little bush bush creatures a great picnic held
  Head cook was the wombat declared
And all danced with delight at the odours
  they smelled
  From the dishes he quickly prepared.
They ate and they ate until nothing remained
  With gusto they gorged every brew
And nicest of all was the pot that contained
  The amazing Uranium Stew.

Then the bunyip announced "There is something I fear
  That will trouble bird, reptile and beast
When in faraway countries the animals hear
  Of our tasty and wonderful feast.
There are dragons in China, peacocks in Japan
  Who hungrier grow by the hour
They will sample our wonderful stew if they can
  To provide themselves prestige and power".

"There's a lion in old England, in Russia a bear
  And an eagle in Yankee land too
And each of these creatures will want a large share
  Of our wondrous Uranium Stew".
Then loud burped the possum, his mouth full of rice
  As he cleaned out the dregs of a pot
"Perhaps it is safer to give them a slice
  Or they might come and eat up the lot".

But the tiger-cat savage snarled "Not on your life
  To surrender like cowards just won't do
Prepare a resistance, there's going to be strife
  If they want our Uranium Stew".
Then up spake the mopoke, a bird very wise

And his eyes in the dark shone like steel
He said "We are foolish, and should realise
   That our secrets we must not reveal".

We have let the world know of the feast
   we have found
   And that knowledge will cause us to rue
For we should have left hidden away in the ground
   The ingredient for making the stew".

The Despoilers

("Japan requires more Australian timber, and the
forests at Newton Boyd are as yet untouched."
Quote by a coastal timber tycoon)

Dark mystic hills and wide plateau
   Where wild the dingo prowls
Weird hollow gums haphazard grow
   The nesting place of owls.
The big rain forest dark and green
   Spreads sheltering and wide
The lyre-bird rare at times is seen
   And small marsupials hide.
Deep gloomy caves in boulders grey
   Where bats and lizards lie
And tiger-cats await their prey
   And eagle-hawks wheel high.

The gleaming river eddies bright
   Down tiny rippling falls
And in the soft enchanting night
   The mournful mopoke calls.
A virgin spot still undestroyed
   By man's destructive hand
How long, how long will Newton Boyd
   Remain unravished land.
A last retreat that soon must go
   Wiped out by axe and gun
As man kills all green things that grow
   And all wild things that run.

How long before the Japanese
   More timber will demand
Then faster still will fall the trees
   To please a foreign land.

The little heritage we hold
    Our childen will not see
The wealthy men who seek more gold
    Will cut down every tree.
How long before the saw and axe
    By greedy powers employed
Lay waste with uncontrolled attacks
    The hills of Newton Boyd.

Computerising

The boffins all claim that a careless mistake
    Is something a modern computer can't make.
You press a few buttons and almost at once
    It quickly enlightens the sorriest dunce.

There is no need for schools to develop young brains
    For all they require the computer explains.
You don't need a pencil, a book or a pad
    To work out your problems computers are glad.

An amazing machine, so say all lazy folk
    No learning is needed, our schools are a joke.
But the people are blind to one small missing link
    The modern computer can't reason or think.

Song of the Reformed Drunk
(Or Grip of the Grape)

Oh sweet is the red Chianti wine
    And sherry endowed with a taste divine
Burgundy white and muscat brown
    At every bar-room in every town
Three Star brandy a wondrous brew
    Pale purple para and claret too
But shun these mockers! There's no escape
    When you find yourself in the Grip of the Grape.

Wine is a traitor full of deceit
    A merciless foe when it has you beat
It addles your brain and you shake with fear
    As ferocious fantods chuckle and leer.
And when terrible jim-jams growl and mutter
    Around your ears as you lie in the gutter
And mysterious mists take human shape
    You'll know you're in the Grip of the Grape.

Fiendish insects frantically hum
    'Til your cranium throbs like an Army drum
Villainous vampire bats come flitting
    And all around you the demons are sitting
Sinister serpents spread wings of fire
    And bunyips bellow from a spectral mire
As they fashion a covering of fiery crepe
    For a brainless bloke in the Grip of the Grape.

Alcohol foul, mankind's great curse
    Steals the brain and empties the purse
Baron or bagman, serf or Lord
    All surrender with one accord.
Keeps it's victims weak and unhealthy
    Degrades the poor and breaks the wealthy.
Drives good men to murder and rape
    Yield not to the deadly Grip of the Grape!

The Smart Australians

There's a school of smart Australians
    With a system hard to beat
They are found in every village
    Country town and city street.
Touring leisurely and guileful from
    the slums to west of Bourke
Fellows always flush with money, but
    who never seem to work.
Suave and shady birds of passage,
    Godless without creed or care
Showing unreserved devotion to the
    pokies, pools and beer.
Tidy, well-fed and financial, though
    they grind no mills for grist.
Simple reader, please inform me just
    how all these coves exist?

After landing unexpected, just as
    quickly they depart
Loafing when the harvest's ready
    or the shearing's due to start.
Some are men who own commitments in
    the shape of kids and wife
Others fancy free and footloose
    Knowing neither strain or strife.
Prominent at weekend races, and the
    dogs again at night
Never lacking for a dollar, future
    prospects always bright.
Shiftless and without ambition,
    just like drones inside a hive
What financial giant enables these
    non-workers to survive?

They were here in the depression,
   flashing coin in store and pub
While the honest toiler battled for
   enough to purchase grub.
When the coppers sought to vag them
   always able to produce
Still around despite inflation, living
   beery, fast and loose
With their free and careless spending
   far in excess of the dole
Flourishing a bulging wallet or a
   neat and tidy roll.
Feeding ruthless on society, like a
   cancerous growth or cyst
Study well my friend the mystery, tell
   me, how do they exist?

Furracabad

(An abandoned mining camp on
the outskirts of Glen Innes)

A rumour arose about lots of tin
   Near the winding creek called Furracabad
The hopeful fossickers quickly moved in
fabulous fortune hoping to win
   But no success these heroes had.
They built crude huts on a stony hill
   And held their claims by miner's right
When the frosty stars were cold and still
On second grade wine they drank their fill
   And howled like dogs in the dead of night.
They lifted mutton from stations around
And bountiful bunnies their hearts made glad
   No longer seeking wealth in the ground
   They worked for wages when work could be found
And survived for a time at Furracabad.

Hitler's war saw the young men enlist
   And to greener pastures went Mum and Dad
Numbers were many and long on the list
And the rag-tag colony ceased to exist
   On the arid acres at Furracabad.
A few old warriors gamely remained
   Holding their places like rates in a hole
   But death and progress quickly ordained
   Their removal; and so they no longer retained
    A desperate existence on pension and dole.
The bulldozers powerful by council were sent
   The carnage they wrecked on the humpies was sad
   And upright citizens smiled in content
   As into the pageant of history went
    the settlement lawless at Furracabad.

(How sad, by Gad! Too bad!)
Up, the rebels.

South of Charleville
(Told to the author by an old ringer)

Bald was the shimmerin' plain and bare
Sunshine hot as a carbide flare
   Weakenin' both heart and will
Homeward bound from a trip below
The borderline where the big mobs go
Through Hebel and Hungerford walkin' slow
   South of Charleville

Pitched the camp in a river bend
Where all night long the mozzies attend
   Takin' of blood their fill
Went to the pub in the dusk of day
With desire to drink and the cash to pay
And the barmaid's smile was seductive and gay
   South of Charleville.

Hair as black as the wing of a crow
Curves just right above and below
   Promisin' joy to fulfil
And her close proximity stirred the lust
That's in mortal man, so it's love or bust
Even with girls beyond faith or trust
   South of Charleville.

Figured her out for an easy mark
Went to a bedroom dirty and dark
   Seekin' the age-old thrill
Taste of grog and odour of sweat
Sound of her laughter haunts me yet
Later I wished we never had met
   South of Charleville.

Woke next morn in the pub's back yard
Layin' on ground both barren and hard
   With a hangover fit to kill
Fallen women with favour to sell
And into the cunnin' snare I fell
Gone was me watch and wallet as well
   South of Charleville.

Trapped by a trick too often played
Like Samson strong by a whore betrayed.
   Doped was the evil swill.
For six long weeks I had sweated it out
Behind starvin' stock in the grip of drought
Left without even the price of a shout
   South of Charleville.

Life grows shorter and memories fade
Often look back on mistakes I made
   And even today I still
Recall her performance lewd and brash
Quick release for both lust and cash
Fires of passion reduced to ash
   South of Charleville.

Ode to a Shearing Flannel

(With apology to Robert Burns)

Worn garment foul, besmirched wi' gore
  Sad relic of the shearin' floor
    Where strain is killin'
In summer weather wringin' wet
  Wi' perspiration; help me yet
    To glean a shillin'.

In winter ere I would retire
  I dried ye oft before the fire
    When dusk was thickenin'
'Til hard ye was as any board
  And bravely every nose ignored
    Your odour sickenin'.

Unwashed, unpressed ye kept me warm
  In flood or famine, fire or storm
    No bounty cravin'
A barricade to halt the pains
  When brawn was needed more than brains
    Where guns were slavin'.

Sad uniform abused and torn
  Dumb witness of the tallies shorn
    In years behind me
When God decides to set me free

  Efficient always, you will be
    The sheet that winds me.

Depression Soup

Half a kerosene-tin
   Handle made of wire
Throw in the ingredients
   Hang it on the fire.
Carrots, peas and onions
   Beans and taters too
From a market garden filched
   Gave flavour to the brew
Skinned galahs and cockatoos
   Simmerin' on the blaze
That was how we made the soup
   In dark depression days.

From the camp to where we toiled
   Where the gum trees droop
We carried on a piece of board
   The steamin' tin of soup
In the board a saw-cut
   So the handle couldn't slip
Walkin' very careful
   To prevent a splash and drip.
Warm it up for dinner
   And sadly I relate
We drank it out of pannikins
   For no-one had a plate.
Any meat was welcome
   Tail of kangaroo
Workin' parts of wombats
   Good old bunnies too.
Knowin' near starvation
   Hungry men would praise
The soup that kerosene-tin held
   In grim depression days.

Now my new electric stove
  Cooks the soup for me
Lots of modern victuals
  Of very high degree
Chicken done with noodles
  Tender high-grade beef
Bones of fish and turtles green
  From the Barrier Reef.
The rich result of progress
  And I never cease to praise
The fact that gone forever
  Are those cruel depresssion days.
When we had to scratch for sustenance
  Like chickens in a coop
And we used a kerosene-tin
  To concoct a feed of soup.

Crossing the Nullabor
(A personal experience)

The Nallabor Plain is a lonely place
   Barren and bare, no greenery
Where wombats scuffle and emus race
   And you see no colourful scenery.
The bitmen road is narrow and hard
   Stretching into infinity
A million flies get under your guard
   No god and no divinity.

Even the lizards look bored and sad
   When the tourists start arriving
And the kangaroos all seem starved and mad
   For a bare existence striving.
Stopped at a roadhouse to get some fuel
   Just as the night was falling
The beer was flat and the heat was cruel
   And the cost was bloody appalling.

Heavy and choking the dust clouds red
   From wind that never stopped blowing
"It's civilisation or bust", I said
   And kept the old van going.
Felt like a man on a sinking ship
   And mate I can tell you truly
The happiest part of the whole damn trip
   Was arriving safe at Kalgoorlie.

The Hawker

Canvas top on the waggonette
   Horses jaded by dust and sweat
Creaking harness and jingling bits
   And 'mid bulky bundles the driver sits.
Western clothes save for turban neat
   And the sandals soft on his dusty feet
Far from his native Pakistan
   That was the hawker, Kharma Kahn.

Tall dark man from across the ocean
   "Sella you the razor, soap and lotion.
"Very good flannel and dungarees
Shearer man he need alla these.
   "Tella your mum good curry I got
Verra cheap saucepan and cooking pot.
   "Verra nice tablecloth white and blue
Shoes and socks for the little ones too."
   Varied merchandise stocked the van
   Of Indian hawker, Kharma Khan.

Made his camp by a shady pool
   On the bank of the river below the school.
Ate his meal as the sun went down
   Curry and rice with chupatties brown.
Faced the East when the dawn was near
   Kneeling low to offer a prayer
To a god who was old ere time began
   True and devout was Kharma Khan.

Days of my youth have forever gone
   But memories of boyhood linger on
In the outback towns no longer is seen
   Kharma Khan with his turban green.
And at times I wonder what fate befell

The tall dark man that we knew so well.
Is he at rest without god or kirk
    In a lonely grave at the back of Bourke?
Or did he go back with a fortune grand
    To his far and mysterious native land?
Accepting the path his god may plan —
    May your sleep be a sound one, Kharma Khan.

Austral Gum

Gaunt and twisted river gum
Through your leaves the bush bees hum
In your shade when full of rum
    Slept the bagmen.

Welcome rest for travellers weary
Drovers tired and shearers beery
Listening to the night wind cheery
    Leaflets stirring.

Hollow spouts where possums camp
Shielded from the cold and damp
Round your trunk the cattle champ
    On the cud contented.

Bushmen in the days gone by
From your fallen folige dry
Made a fire their food to fry
    And boil the billy.

Pioneers of early days
Of your timber sang high praise
Home and shed it helped to raise
    On the new selections.

In the floods your roots stood sound
Men cut off by water found
Safety above the ground
    In your branches.

Sheltering both man and beast
West and north and south and east
Of true Aussies not the least
    Is the gum-tree.

217

Flight of the Paddington Bear

The Parliament sat with expression severe
    Deciding the fate of poor Mick
And shrouded in gloom was the Paddington Bear
    A creature unhappy and sick.
He said, "No-one wants me in this rugged land
    'Tis no wonder I'm lonely and blue
Koalas and Teddies they quite understand
    And they love little Yankee Bears too."

"But the statesmen all view me with horror and fear
    For foggy old London I yearn
Where a welcome awaits for the Paddington Bear
    If they'll only allow my return.
The strange Birds of Government continue to squawk
    The Peacock is noisy and shrill
And talons of anger are spread by the Hawke
    As he studies requests for a kill."

"A bucket of whitewash is needed, 'tis said
    But the Liberal Birds do not agree
Any hope for my sponsor it seems has gone dead
    And his future a hard one could be.
I'm a small docile bear of good standing and note
    Who obeys regulations and laws
Unlike the big bear in the shaggy red coat
    Who is testing his long nuclear claws.

"By the foes of our freedom his praises are sung
    He is patiently waiting his chance
And of little importance will be Mr Young
    If the Red Bear decides to advance.
Should he go on the rampage no foe will he spare
    And the carnage will turn the world sick
So good statesmen have mercy on Paddington Bear
    And provide reinstatement for Mick."

Prostitutes in a Mining Camp

For us no mansion bright with wealth abounding
   Crude comforts few our masters hard ordain
Painted and preened with poverty surrounding   In sordid
huts of tin we entertain.
The red lamps glow, the desert night is silent
   A chill wind rises as the hour grows late
Where lust and shame combine in conflict violent
   To man's debauchery sold we patient wait.

Furtive they come with wild eyes dulled by liquor
   From excavations deep within the ground
Propelled by old desires that flame and flicker
   Soldiers of toil unsung and unrenowned.
With conscience cast aside we sate their longing
   Though from our act no pleasure we derive
While ghosts of what we might have been coming thronging
   To haunt us 'til the daylight hours arrive.

No future fine for us, but night unending
   Our stigma-tarnished lives no goal may find
Surrendering swift to sin, no hand defending
   Shunned by society in a world unkind.
But oft we dream that God will mercy render
   And look upon us with foregiveness bright
Finding us all a lover true and tender
   To lift us from the Pit that holds us tight.

Mandy's Cat

Above my humble little home
    the moon is shining bright
Now swift and silent something moves,
    a shadow in the night.
It's eyes are gleaming ghostly green,
    a creature sleek and fat
That often uninvited comes,
    it's Mandy's ginger cat.

I don't know what he's looking for
    there are no she-cats here,
He doesn't smoke or gamble
    and he doesn't go for beer.
He doesn't pry or interfere
    in anybody's life
He never skites or gossips
    and he never causes strife.

He's quite an asset to our street
    He cleans up every mouse
He doesn't scratch the garden up
    or come inside the house
To grab things off the table
    every time you look away
For Mandy's cat trustworthy is
    not like some folk today.

They try at every chance they see
    to touch you for a buck
But never want to know you
    when you're running out of luck.
And closing off my rhyme, I think
    it's very plain to see
That Mandy's little ginger cat
    a good true friend will be.

The Pastoral Dispute
1983

It's on again! The shearers all are striking
   Once more opposing arbitration rules
The wider comb just isn't to their liking
   So it's shed the dungarees and drop the tools
I remember past disputes and tempers wearing
   I am glad old mates I'm not involved with you
The narrow comb I couldn't fill when shearing
   With a wider one I don't know what I'd do.

Here in Glen Innes town each pastoral faction
   Display belligerence of a very stubborn form
With dissolusioned shearers ripe for action
   And graziers standing firm to meet the storm.
All over shearing tools of different making
   The arbiters negotiate day and night
And men involved deplorable steps are taking
   To prove their point and win
     the senseless fight.

I went up town today, a haircut seeking
   From Bob Morton, a tonsorialist of skill
He was silent to the point of hardly speaking
   And appeared the victim sad of fortune ill.
A pessimistic word he seldom utters
   But 'twas plain his sense of humour now had fled
He was closing shop and putting up the shutters
   "I'm going out of business, Garv", he said.

"I placed a wider comb upon the clippers
   A foolish thing to do, I must declare
Now the shearer men and all their wives
   and nippers
   Refuse to let me cut a single hair".

Across the road I went to see George Correy
  A barber who is held in great respect
But George alas, related a sad story
  For his hopes of any future work were wrecked.

He said "It seems my barbering days are ended
  'I'm closing down the shop and going home
For the graziers on whom much trade depended
  Discovered that I use a narrow comb".

So listen to my question, gentle hearers
  As each hour dissention grows across our land
And tell me, will the barbers join the shearers
  Or with the graziers and their cohorts stand.
I dislike long hair, and though the frosts
  are nippy
  To scruffiness I wish not to descend
Each passing day I look more like a hippy
  And I hope to God the pastoral dispute will end.

Wet Camp

A wind from the north begins to blow
   The boughs of the box-trees lifting
Hungry cattle are feeding slow
Darkness heightens the camp-fire's glow
   As dreary sleet comes drifting.
No need to hobble the nags tonght
   The fences need no rewiring
Round the small reserve that holds us tight
Sleep without worry 'til morning light
   The day was long and tiring.
Tighten the fly and dig a drain
   So the water won't run under
Heavier now is the misty rain
The horse bells sound a ragged refrain
   No lightning thank God, or thunder.

Darkie sits on a box-tree's bole
   Swarthy and pensive study
Lighting his pipe with a camp-fire coal
Longing for home with heart and soul
   Tattered and worn and muddy.
Skeeter mourns for a girl he knew
   Way out west at Brewarrina
Had the idea her heart was true
'Til unexpected away she flew
   With a dark and handsome foreigner.
Paddy leans on a shaft of the dray
   New-chum fresh from Killarney
Ever so often his sad thoughts stray
To his small green land so far away
   With its banshees, elves and blarney.

London Bob stands lanky and lean
   Watching the camp-fire flicker

English gentleman once he's been
Now debarred from the social scene
  By unsated desire for liquor.
Duncan has cooked some spuds and beef
  Steam from the boiler rises
Flavour the tea with a green gum lead
Forget for a while the toil and grief
  Of droving enterprises.
Men of a calling hard and drear
  Find small pleasures contenting
  Dreaming of township lights and beer
  What are MY thoughts as night draws near
  I'd rather refrain from commenting.

Stockwhip on the Wall
(Lament of an old Ringer)

Heavy on my shoulders hang the years
   Life recedes as sinks the setting sun
Far too old for joy, too old for tears
   Little whip, my day like yours is done.
Worn like me, with willow handle bended
   Frayed the greenhide plait and short the fall
Reminder of a way of life now ended
When down lonely tracks the cattle wended
   Little stockwhip hangin' on the wall.

Sunlight shinin' on an arid plain
   Lanky coastal bullocks walkin' slow
Just a memory flittin' back again
   Of the life and times I used to know.
When the wide bush held no ties to bind me
   Ridin' free of regulations small
Though my young years lie behind me
You're the one thing to remind me
   Little stockwhip hangin' on the wall.

Windy winter days and frosty dawns
   Starry nights and blazin' summer suns
Closer draws the end; my tired heart mourns
   For the old bush life on western runs.
Round the camp-fire's blaze I hear the laughter
   Of the rough old mates I well recall
But their ranks are now diminished
And their day like ours is finished
   Little stockwhip hangin' on the wall.

No true stockmen ride the runs today
   Pitt Street ringers mounted up on bikes

225

Muster in an automated way
   Dinkum, I have never seen the likes
Now no more we hear the horse bells ringin'
   Accompanyin' the curlew's crazy call
Or the sighin' the night-wind bringin'
To our ears the watchman's singin'
   Little stockwhip hangin' on the wall.

Within it's own inertia's sticky bog
   The outback sinks in decadence I fear
Sometimes when in an alcoholic fog
   I long again for days of yesteryear.
The old Australian ways are long forgotten
   And foreign combines soon will own us all
And the free life that I cherished
In the march of time has perished
   Little stockwhip hangin' on the wall.

Uncertain Runners

He cut it out in thirty-six
  With the flags out forty feet
I told my good supporters
  "Here's a horse that can't be beat."
We backed him on the Saturday
  And our coin went down the drain
He only ran a moderate third
  But his lapse I can explain.
In every race he started
  He just wouldn't do his best
He left his good form on the track
  As the clockers could attest

*   *   *   *   *   *

In every walk of life today
  Where you do your best to win
You will meet the slick performer
  Who can easily get you in.
With his confident approaches
  Working every pub in town
He will look a certain winner
  'Til you put the money down.
And you find this type of runner
  When the future's looking black
And he's asked to make an effort
  Always leaves it on the track.

227

Ode to Animal Lovers
(Of the R.S.P.C.A.)

A stray cat was a nuisance, so I quickly
   put him down
   With a well-directed bullet clean and fast
My swift and needy action caused authority to frown
   From the R.S.P.C.A. I copped a blast.
"You brutal man, you killed a cat, how could you be so
bad?
   Your type of criminal should be put away
The thought of wanton cruelty makes me quite
   depressed and sad"
   Said the lady from the R.S.P.C.A.

I said, "My gallant lady, your costumery appeals
   I am sure the clothes designers would concur
Does it make you sad to think about
   the little baby seals
   That were bashed to death to make
     your coat of fur?"
Do you feel a tearful sorrow for
   the poor old kangaroo
   That was slaughtered for your fashionable purse
The feathers in your headgear from a parrot
   red and blue.
   Was the killing of a feline any worse?"

"The carpet snake who gave his hide
   to decorate your shoes
   Dragged protesting from his warm and hollow tree
I must inform you madam, that you haven't any clues
   You are unenlightened, that is plain to see".
Very silent grew the lady, realising she was caught
   And ashamedly she hied herself away
And ever since that meeting I have ceased
   to give a thought
   To some members of the R.S.P.C.A.

A Wet Shed
(When the rain is endless on the land)

Writers seek to glamourize the shearin'
  Most of them will never understand
How monotonous it becomes and wearin'
  When the rain is endless on the land.

*   *   *   *   *   *

Rise and shine again oh noble shearer
  Dark and gloomy skies a morbid sight
Wet and greasy garments wait the wearer
  Downpour drummin' ceaseless through the night.
Clammy dungarees and dirty flannel
  Backaches activated by the rain
Water runnin' wild in every channel
  Spreadin' like an ocean on the plain.
Sticky ewes that need deodourizing'
  Gluey mud congealin' on yer boots
  Rouseabouts show energy surprisin'
Pools of water formin' round the chutes.
  Hungry sheep too long incarcerated
Shearers leanin' weary on the stand
  Union matters heatedly debated
When the rain is endless on the land.

Toilets that are sore in need of drainin'
  Musterers sad and wet as half-drowned crows
In the crib the cranky cook complainin'
  Ambitious learner thinkin' up new blows
On his bunk the drunken ringer mutters
  Tortured by a nightmare dark and deep
Centipedes go sailin' down the gutters
  Possums in the roof upset yer sleep.

229

Swarm of moths around the lamp paradin'
    Frogs that nightly form a noisy band
    Shearin' is a dreary job degradin'
    When the rain is endless on the land.
Mangy kelpies overgorged on offal
    Rouseabouts grow fatter every day
Huts disorderly as any brothel
    Time a feller gave the game away.

*   *   *   *   *   *

Writers always glamourize the shearin'
    Plain to see they'll never understand
How monotonous it becomes and wearin'
    When the rain is endless on the land.

Vale Boozer
(A true friend passes)

Come round all men who love a dog
and listen to my rhyme
   For Boozer headed west to-day
   into the mists of time
No more he prowls the watercourse
amid the rustling sags
   His toothless jaws are closed for good
   his tail no longer wags.

No claim to beauty could he make
his scaley paws were hard
   His rheumy eyes were dull with age
   his hide was battle scarred.

He lived a long and carefree life
'til he was old and grey
   Te Mona doesn't seem the same
   since Boozer passed away.
He wouldn't muster cattle up
he wouldn't muster sheep
   At times his sinful laziness
   would cause old Dunc to weep.

But he was true and faithful from
the day he was a pup
   And used to make an awful row
   when Duncan tied him up.
A mightly lover in his youth
if any bitch was near
   And many cross-bred pups he sired
   Of shape and colour queer.

But old and toothless he became
for time shows no regard
    No longer could he chew a bone
    or tucker that was hard.
Cruel rheumatism racked his joints
and oft he cried at night
    But still he didn't like to let
    his master out of sight.

So when he finally racked his cue
old Dunc was close to tears
    The ringer and his dog were mates
    for fourteen happy years.

          ★   ★   ★   ★   ★   ★

But when the sun to westward drops
And daylight slowly dies
    I think perhaps 'neath Duncan's bed
    Old Boozer's spirit lies.
Displaying all the faultless faith
he held from day to day
    Te Mona doesn't seem the same
    since Boozer passed away.

          ★   ★   ★   ★   ★   ★

Australian (?)

My wireless plays a happy song
All day long
It's made in Hong Kong.
My typewriter as you can see
comes from far off Italy
I wonder just why this should be
 I am Australian.

I own a natty litle car
Made in Tokyo afar
Just like all the others are.
My rifle bears a Yankee stamp
The small tent sheltering my camp
Is made in England like my Lamp
 I am Australian.

Fat on Grecian wine I grow
Chili sauce for which I go
Is produced in Mexico.
German pens and ink I ply
Every T-shirt that I buy
Bears a brand "Chicago High"
 I am Australian.

All our Governments daily cower
On their knees to foreign power
We grow weaker by the hour.
In a land betrayed for gain
Could some master mind explain
Just how long I will remain
 Australian.

Deep Respect
(Or bitter experience?)

"You win respect", the fat man said,
   "by working long and hard
   A loafer who unwilling shows is held
     in small regard.
"I started on a pound a week and saved up every bob
   And won respect from everyone by sticking
     to the job
"When honest sweat upon your brow is plain
   for all to see
   You'll be respected far and near by wealthy men
     like me."
A fat and flabby creature soft,
   with badly swollen joints
   He looked as if the only work he did
     was working points.
But I took his word in simple faith
   and laboured every day
   And strange to say, the more I worked
     the less he cared to pay.

If you're mug enough to stand it,
   then the moneyed folk around
   Will work you like a draught-horse and then
     send you to the pound.
So sadly I decided as I rolled my heat-wave swag
   That respect from wealthy people never fills
     the tucker bag.
They claim they found security by working
   day and night.
   But if you check their history
     it's a bloody lot of skite.
And their fortune was inherited,

or gained by luck or crime
But now they have the money
   they command respect sublime.
And the way to be respected I have
  long decided now
Is to make a lot of money,
   and it doesn't matter how.

The Ti-Tree

'The modest ti-tree thickly grows
  Along the mountain creeks in rows.
Though cool and shady it may be
  It can't produce a leaf of ti.
The hippy communes love its shade
  No Ti-shirts for them has it made
Upon its foliage dark and green
  No golfer's ti-s are ever seen
And should the traveller thirsty be
  It can't pour out a cup of ti.

When scarlet blossoms make it pretty
  It grows no ti-bags, more's the pity.
No sobering ti it ever serves
  To calm the boozer's shattered nerves.

Good friends, from ignorance please make me-free
And tell me why it's called the ti-tree.

Gee-Gees and Girls
(A comparison by an old ringer)

Wouldn't win a prize at any show
   Too ungainly for a lady's hack
Floppy ears and belly hangin' low
   Donkey head and hollow back.
Never sees a curry-comb or brush
   No exotic fodder, only grass
But on stormy nights when cattle rush
   He shows his class.

Standin' hipshot in the darkness deep
   Wise and patient at his job
New-chums all would reckon he's asleep
   But he's watchin' the mob.
Ready when the bushy ones break camp
   He gets movin' with surprisin' speed
Scatterin' the dewy grasses damp
   Makin' for the lead.

Dashin' through the night on rough terrain
   Where the wild stampede disturbs the dust
Just sit tight and gives him lots of rain
   And your trust.
All his efforts seem to prove indeed
   An idea I've got
Be it faithful girl or faithful steed
   Looks don't mean a lot.

Let the gaudy types of prancin' past
   They are seldom strong in times of strife
Get an honest one that's made to last
   Be it horse or wife.

Bi-Centenary Blues

It's nineteen-eighty-eight, the Tall Ships sail
    Like Phillip's fleet once sailed to Botany Bay
The spirits of our pioneers prevail
    Proud of our country we should be today.
Here in my dark and lonely city den
    I sit and watch the morning light arrive
Gone are the fearful hours of darkness when
    The cruel nocturnal creatures roam and thrive.

Beneath an awning lies a drunken sot
    A weary harlot smokes in ill-content
It's safe to bet the poor jade hasn't got
    Enough to pay the bludger and the rent.
A homosexual makes a haunting sound
    Seeking a lover with its mournful cry
A timid dead-beat moves to higher ground
    From dew-drenched lane and park no longer dry.

The thieves and muggers all have fled the night
    The unemployed awaken without hope
A drug supplier bold with prospects bright
    Searches for foolish clients who crave for dope.
A stray dog overturns a garbage tin
    The awful smell befouls the early morn
A bootless hippy with a bearded grin
    Surveys the offerings in a house of porn.

Loud from an all-night disco comes the howls
    Of teenage kids with brains impaired by "pot"
The metho drinkers sit with eyes like owls
    Amid the debris on a vacant lot.
The night-shift leaves the massage parlour bright
    Gone for a day of rest at God Knows Where

Exhausted by a sad and sinful night
　　Too tired to hope and too far gone to care.

A police car crawls along the lightening street
　　Weary and dissolusioned seem the cops
Trying their hardest crime and vice to beat
　　Fighting a battle grim that never stops.
Lucky are we who reap the rich reward
　　Two hundred years of progress has supplied
Salute our governments wise with great accord
　　Cheer for our bi-centenary with pride.

Ringer's Requiem

(Michael Dunn, an Irish stockman
drowned in a flooded Queensland creek
at the end of last century.)

Hardly a funeral well attended
Rough and ready the sermon rendered
    Tears were none
"May God receive yer", the drover pleaded
"Always there when yer most wuz needed
"Rebel yer wuz by no rules impeded
    Mickey Dunn".

No priest, no rosary beads, no hearse
Coffin a blanket for wear the worse
    Life's race run
Hats in hand and booted and spurred
We sadly watched your corpse interred
Perhaps unspoken prayers were heard
    Mickey Dunn.

Mystery migrant aloof and silent
Never offensive, never violent
    Sought no fun
At a risky crossing you copped a clout
From a drifting log in the flood, no doubt
Dead as a duck when we fished you out
    Mickey Dunn.

Why did you leave old Ireland's shore
Was it because you were poverty poor?
    Future none
Dinkum mate on the droving track
Shared your money when times were slack
Never divulged why you couldn't go back
    Mickey Dunn.

Did you cross the path of the I.R.A.
And headed South for a getaway?
    Cut and run
Were you a lover with heart untrue
Was there a colleen, possibly two
Left in the lurch your sins to rue?
    Mickey Dunn.

Here in a land of little gain
Life was hard but you didn't complain
    In storm or sun
Game as the Paddies always are
Sought no fortune, followed no star
And your God was a glass on the shanty bar
    Mickey Dunn.

Knew better times, I'm game to bet
Far from the Outback's toil and sweat
    Ireland's son
Parents perhaps in County Clare
Sisters and brothers in 'ould Kildare'
None of them now of your fate aware
    Mickey Dunn.

Sins and virtues for aye dispelled
Safe are the secrets you always held
    Hopes unwon
Peaceful sleep on the sandhill's crown
Dream of the meadows in Country Down
Will old Saint Peter smile or frown?
    Mickey Dunn.

Fairy Folk
(An Irish Fantasy)

On summer nights in Kerry when the mystic moon is
mellow.
    You will see the goblins dancing, wagging pointed ears
and sharp
In little boots with turned-up toes and garments green
and yellow
    While the banshee and the badger play the fiddle
and the harp.
In a world of Gaelic fantasy where fairy feet are flitting
    And the bluebells ring a chorus in their brilliant azure
coats
While on dandelions and toadstools cunning leprechauns
are sitting
    And the rooks compose an audience with the jackdaws
and the stoats.

Fairy folk of fitful fancy, still maintaining old tradition
    In a land of deep emotions and secure religious ties
Borne of weird and wondrous witchery, kept alive by
superstition
    Elfin creatures small created by the minds of ancients
wise.
So when summer moons are shining take the road that
leads to Kerry
    Amid myriad magic cultures seek again the old
romance
And the happiness of earlier years when life was gay and
merry
    You will live again your childhood when you watch the
goblins dance.

Out of a Place

Two Kerrymen to Curragh course
  Went hopefully to back a horse.
Said Mick "Begad, the odds are nice
  Twenty-five to one the price".
"Each way I'll bet", the bookie said
And this caused Pat to scratch his head,
While Mick displayed a puzzled look
  And doubtfully surveyed the 'book'.

"Come on", the son of Judah cried
  "The track is good, the odds are wide.
"Perhaps it is your lucky day
  Step up and back the horse each way".
Said Pat "I notice in this place
  There's just one way the horses race
In one direction, never two
  Begorra I won't bet with you.
'Tis certain, Ike, ye will not pay
  If ours goes round the other way".

Irish Migrant Girls

From the slums of Dublin town, and
    the hills of Country Down
They migrated to a country wild and wide
    Where the outback's sweeping fastness
      in Australia's endless vastness
Gave a promise that their homeland had denied.
    From the bogs of Tipperary, Biddy
      Norah, Kate and Mary
Fleeing famine where the crops had failed to grow
    Trying vainly to be cheerful
      at the parting sad and tearful
Sailing south to where the Austral sunsets glow.
    So by homestead, hut and tent, weary
      years of toil they spent
Knowing long incessant hardship day by day
    Speech and manners rude and rough
      but undaunted spirit tough
The migrant girls from Ireland far away.

Hard they slaved and loved and mated
    and strange stories they related
As the yoke of endless servitude they bore
    And they dreamed of Cork and Kerry, where
      the fairy-folk make merry
In the 'ould sod', left behind for evermore.
    Through the dust clouds hot and blinding
      where the waggon-wheels were grinding
They maintained a perseverance stout and true
    Tireless in the summer swelter
      by the tents that formed a shelter
For the fettlers where the line was going through.
    On the lonely western streams, and
      the plains where saltbush gleams

It was seldom peace and comfort came their way
   There was little time to dally by
     the wash-tub and the galley
For the migrant girls from Ireland far away.

   So they battled grim privation
     in the conquest of a nation
Though the wealthy man their loyalty denies
   But they helped to win the land
     daughters of a rebel band
For the Fenian blood no quick surrender cries.
   Though to history they have gone
     Still descendants carry on
With a preference strong for stout instead of wine
   Bred from Kate and Maggie Dooley
     Sally Bourke and Biddy Hooley
Standing stoutly where their forebears blazed the line.
   From the eastern coast to Perth
     long they proved their rugged worth
Showing fortitude to battle sad dismay
   With a smile for every neighbour
     and the will to love and labour
The migrant girls from Ireland far away.

A Plea to Eire

The thrush gives out his merry trills
   The meadow lark joins in
For Spring has come to Kerry hills
   And though the grass is thin
And sheep and cattle lank and lean
   Cold winter-time departs
The sycamores are budding green
   To gladden Irish hearts.

The soft rain comes like bitter tears
   That mourn for Ireland's plight
May God recall the troubled years
   And all the wrongs make right.
Dismiss the bigots of each creed
   Whose ways are small and mean
And may the Orange cast its seed
   In peace amid the Green.

Toil on, O gallant sons of Eire
   One day perhaps you'll see
The grand 'Ould Sod of trouble clear
   From strife forever free.
In unity try hard to stand
   Let fancied wrongs depart
For spring has come to Ireland
   And hope is in each heart.

A Kerry Legend

He had to be ninety years at least
   A tough old Gael with a pipe of clay
A flood of legends his tongue released
   And here is a tale he told that day.

       ★   ★   ★   ★   ★   ★

There's a spot in Kerry where a banshee lives
   By a sycamore clump in a patch of mud
And at night a terrible shriek he gives
   That would curdle and freeze the devil's own blood
All day long he hides and scans
   A bend in the road where the earth's polluted
By the bodies of several black and tans
   That patriot Paddies executed.

When their spirits seek to escape at night
   "Traitors and cowards" the banshee screams
And they shiver and shake with endless fright
   Guilt and repentance haunting their dreams.
Tools of tyrants exploiting the poor
   Scum of the English gutters were they
A uniform shameful and hated they wore
   And I tell you me boys, you'll see the day

When then the grand ould sod will once again
   Stand free from the merciless laws imposed
Broken will be the usurpers chain
   And the good green flag will wave unopposed.

The Great Potato Famine
(and it's aftermath)

The Paddies migrated to foreign soil
    Because in Ireland there wasn't a spud
They sought to escape from slavery and toil
And the English tyrants who starve and despoil
    So they caused a migratory flood

They converged in thousands on foreign strands
    In pursuit of a beckoning star
Strong and willing of hearts and hands
They left their mark on the Yankee lands
    By constructing the U.P.R.

On lumber camps in Canada's snows
    Where rich men ground the grist
In tropical swamps where fever glows
And Austral acres where saltbush grows
    They were tops on the labour list.

Stoic and game till the fight was won
    At their best when the odds were great
Never a job that was badly done
Where the lands were conquered and nations won
    The Paddies pulled their weight.

From the 'ould sod' still they migrate today
    Sons of the rebel blood
Born to battle and bred to stay
From the small green country drifting away
    Because in Ireland there wasn't a spud.

Neglected Heroes

I took a trip to Charing Cross on a
   wintry day and raw
Lord Nelson's statue stands there,
   and regretfully I saw
How high and cold his column is,
   and sad it was to note
That England's naval hero bold wore
   no warm overcoat.

But resolute and firm he was as when
   wounded sore he lay
On the Victory's shattered quarter-deck
   at grim Trafalgar Bay.
'Twas a sad and careless oversight by
   every British peer
To leave Lord Nelson in the rain
   with no overcoat to wear.

And in the bar that afternoon
   I thought with deep regret
Of all the unsung heroes who go coatless
   in the wet
Who when wounded by misfortune
   never wilt or cry enough
Life the hero of Trafalgar when
   the odds he faced were tough.

Men who fight a willing battle
   but who never reach the top
In their dotage sadly lacking for
   a place to eat and flop.
And our statesmen fat and placid
   ought to spend a little more
On constructing homes and shelters
   for the ancient and the poor.

Shearer's Farewell
To His Sweetheart

I hope dear girl you'll understand, I'm tired
  of weekly payment
  Niggard pittance for my efforts at a menial job in town
Striking meek ingratiating pose attired in city raiment
  Servile slave to boring custom, just a poor obedient
clown.
For it's Southward of the city streets
  the southern spring is waking
And the shearers all are heading down
    the 'Bidgee and the Bland
Filled with hale and happy hearts to face
  a wearying undertaking
And the old life ceaseless beckons,
    so I hope you'll understand.

You can boast of Continental meals, processed and
dehydrated
  Let me have the shearer's kitchen,
    giving welcome every day
Where with every kind of provender the stove
  is always weighted.
  Freshly cooked and fragrant dishes,
    not the stale junk you take away.

Earthy industry unhampered by small rule and regulation
  Where the worker has the right to have his say
    and make demand
So I'm taking off tomorrow to a manlier occupation
  For the Southern sheds are starting
    and I hope you'll understand.

In the city's walls imprisoned I grow indolent
and weary
Where true faith and Christianity
like pallid ghosts have fled
I am longing for companionship of old mates
bright and beery
And the humorous yarns they prattle at the bar
and in the shed.

So away from strife and squalor for a while
at least I'm going
Where the men who toil beside you show
a willing heart and hand
For the past I know is calling where
the southern streams are flowing
And the Southern hills are waking,
and I hope you'll understand.

Human torrent ceaseless rushing like a
flooded western river
Unenlightened city minds obsessed
by ignorance and greed
And my heart seeks silent valleys
where the spreading gum boughs quiver
And it's time that I was going
where the outback pathways lead.

So a fond farewell, the track of fate
divided lies before us
For 'twas long ago the Red God chose
to mark me with his brand
On the hills the men are mustering
and the kelpies raise a chorus
I'll be on the train tomorrow,
and I know you'll understand.

The Bush Museum

Where fossickers follow fortune's dream
    And the fabulous opals glow
Go to the Lightning Ridge Museum
    Out where the wilgas grow.
There is recorded an era past
    Relics of yesteryear
Gathered from acres void and vast
    To promote our heritage dear.

Gadgets from every walk of life
    Shovel, sickle and plough
Telling of struggle, strain and strife
    In a nation conquered now.
Horsebells and hobbles, saddles and packs
    The tools of the horseback days
Seen no longer on western tracks
    Where the big mobs used to graze.

Old recordings and gramophones
    Unknown to the youth of today
As they mesmerised stand where a pop-star moans
    Watching him shudder and sway.
Concertinas that entertained
    At many a shearing shed
Pianos and fiddles that plinked and strained
    When a groom and his bride were wed.

Rockers and sieves from a mining camp
    Where diggers dreamed of success
Water-bags carried on many a tramp
    Handpieces, shears and press.
Obsolete harvesters gone to rust
    Since earlier farming days

251

When the hooves of the Clydesdales stirred the dust
  Machines that the old hands praise.

Souvenirs sacred from days of yore
  In the Bush Museum you will find
When the face of Australia was hard and raw
  A challenge to strong mankind.
So visit the Bush Museum, my friends
  Where our heritage lingers on
And a spirit of reverence close attends
  From an era past and gone.

Riding Rocky Ned

(Told by an old Ringer)

Yer meet some dreamers in the bush
   Exaggerators too
Bare-knuckle pugs and shearin' guns
   Who put three hundred through.
They bore yer stiff and bash yer lug
   Until yer nearly weep
You bet they never had a fight
   Or never shore a sheep.
There's axemen, wrestlers, big-gun cooks
   And blokes who've cut the cane
They tell yer of their mighty deeds
   In boastful words profane.

They skite for hours without a spell
   'Til yer nearly off yer head
But the biggest liar is the bloke
   Who once rode Rocky Ned.
Tom Hanley's famous buckjump horse
   The star-turn of the show
All noted riders bit the dust
   Each time they had a go.
Only one man ever rode him
   Up in Moree town one night
A policeman named Jack Riley
   Who was not a bloke to skite.

Then Thorpe McConville bought him
   And the game old moke bucked on
Until the years caught up with him
   And Rocky Ned was gone.
Now senile sinners old and weak
   And oft confined to bed

253

Will tell yer how in times gone by
   They mastered Rocky Ned.
They spin a wild embellished yarn...
   "Be god, I showed 'em how!"
But the only thing they ever rode
   Was a cocky farmer's plough.

The blokes who claim they rode the horse
   If yer got 'em mustered up
Would outnumber the attendance
   At the bloody Melbourne Cup.
They never cease to tell yer
   'Bout their deeds of long ago
They think they've got yer kidded
   But the knowin' blokes all know.
And still around those Western towns
   Where morning suns rise red
You'll find the windy skite who claims
   He once rode Rocky Ned.

Saveloys

Oft in the depression years
Working men were close to tears
  When there was no meat
When a sheep could not be lifted
Pockets were for pennies sifted
  For a substitute to eat...
    Saveloys.

Tuppence each down at the Greek's
Been in stock sometimes for weeks
  Dehydrated bad
Sister, brother, dad and mother
Shared the starvers with each other
  All the grub we had...
    Saveloys.

Dry and hard as bricks in Hell
Eat 'em raw or boil 'em well
  Old hands used to state
They were made of dogs and cats
Tongues of pigs and tails of rats
  But we bravely ate...
    Saveloys.

Constipation cruel inflicted
Just the same I was addicted
  Couldn't get enough
Stomach pains too often followed
When with hunger sharp we swallowed
  Bags of mystery tough...
    Saveloys.

Good times now are on the land
Still we find them in demand
  Frozen, fresh and new
Still some doubt what they contain
Manufacturers won't explain
  But who cares? Let's chew...
    Saveloys.

255

An Obvious Fact

The shearer loafs in the public bar
  Eyeing the world through beer-induced mists
And he always complains that the squatters are
  Bloated Capitalists.
The squatter sups in his castle hall
  From drinking Scotch he never desists
And he reckons the shearers are one and all
  Despicable Communists.

*   *   *   *   *   *   *

Now if the shearer inherited pelf
  The working class he would never assist
Because he would now consider himself
  A bloated Capitalist.
If the squatter was stripped of all worldly sum
  And his mills no longer would grind any grist
He would join the Union and quickly become
  A despicable Communist.

256

Six Feet Under

(An Agnostic's argument)

Do Bible and clergy provide the solution?
Or was Darwin right about evolution?
    I often wonder.
But you safely can wager any amount on
One thing; a small wooden box you can count on
    Six feet under.

Millionaires and demagogues greedy
Through whose ambitions the poor and needy
    Are torn asunder.
With tarnished gold buy respectability
And like us all reach a final tranquility
    Six feet under.

Politicians who live by deceit
Criminals no system can ever defeat
    Who rape and plunder.
Obsessed by a force that no power can delay
Surrender at last their dispensable clay
    Six feet under.

Dullard and genius, dreamer and grafter
Hoping perhaps there exists a hereafter
    Through life we blunder.
When the reaper relentless our shroud has unfurled
We all are assured of a place in the world
    Six feet under.

Leave Him In The Dog Yard

(A parody by Garv, with sincere apologies to Messrs.
Dixon and Dusty)

He's a nuisance on the place
Hasn't any style or grace
    His type of horse can send a feller grey
A treacherous sort to moke
He was never properly broke
    So leave him in the dogsmeat yard today.
Not a strong and robust steed
Just a poor and boney weed
    Though we fed him bales of Riverina hay
    We bought him corn from Gatton
    But he simply wouldn't fatten
So leave him in the dogsmeat yard today.

A smart and cunning wretch
And an awful rogue to catch
    Last night he kicked his mate the baldy bay
Just watch him dodge and sidle
When he sees you with a bridle
    So leave him in the dogsmeat yard today.
At the show he wins no prize
And he's dumped a lot of guys
    Who climbed aboard his back in hopes to stay
Lance Skuthorpe tried to do him
But the bludger up and threw him
    So leave him in the dogsmeat yard today.

He knows every devilish trick
And he loves to strike and kick
    I'll be more than happy when he's far away
Where his hooves will clump and clatter

258

Down the ramp at Parramatta
　　So leave him in the dogsmeat yard today.
In a greyhound's stomach dark
He will race at Harold Park
　　And never mind the RSPCA
And the knackery profiteers
For his soul will shed no tears
　　So leave him in the dogsmeat yard today.

The Bittern

The bittern in his plumage brown
   Inhabits swamp and marsh
Like orators of high renown
   His boring voice is harsh.
He makes a meal from frogs and worms
   On long lagoons at night
His deep disturbing cry confirms
   That he's a Bushland skite.

Just like a common type you strike
   In pub bars every day
A small and scruffy little tyke
   Who has too much to say.
And new-chums friendless and forlorn
   By terror stark are smitten
When nightly on the breeze is borne
   The booming of the bittern.

He minds no mud and cloying ooze
   Or blinding rains that pelter
No self-respecting bird would use
   The bittern's nest for shelter
A crazy platform hidden well
   Of small sticks ill-constructed
Beneath it, causing awful smell
   His toilet is conducted.

Although he thinks his loud bombast
   The predators has beaten
You'll often find his feathers cast
   Where fox or cat has eaten.
So little men take heed this day
   To what the Scribe has written
And never have too much to say
   Or you'll be like the bittern.

The Nuclear Beast

The Nuclear Beast has slumbered
  Since the advent of his birth
But his tentacles far-reaching
Strangle every land on earth.
And the gluttonous money moguls
  Playing hard for higher stakes
Care but little for the reckoning
  If the Nuclear Beast awakes
To spread a frightful carnage
  With his flag of wrath unfurled
And leave behind him smouldering
  Wreckage of the modern world.

The Nuclear Beast is restless
  A fact that few can see
By day and night he grumbles
  For the powers to set him free.
And the selfish little people
  Rushing on in greedy haste
Will regret in final moments
  When they see the land laid waste.
Ignorant and uncomprehending
  By the ruthless bought and sold
They will know too late their error
  When the beast roams uncontrolled.

He will spare not his creators
  They like lesser men can die
As like rats they run for cover
  From the fall-out drifting by.
Take a firm stand little people
  In all corners of the world
For the time arrives for action
E'er the holocaust is hurled.
Drop your apathetic outlook
  Move before the war-gods feast
Cast aside all regulations
  And destroy the Nuclear Beast!!

261

Kerry Girl

Sad and grey the cloud canopy creeping
    Like a shroud spread forlorn and austere
Ruffled ocean salt tears ceaseless weeping
    Where incessant the waves lap the pier.
With sincerity strong let me tell you
    As the moment arrives to depart
'Tis with sad soul depressed I farewell you
    And a place I'll reserve in my heart
Indistinct on the wharf grow the faces
    Lost at last in the wet misty spray
Though I journey to far distant places
    I'll remember you, Kitty O'Shea.

Kerry spring and blue mountains were towering
    Where the rooks uttered noisy protest
As they flapped in the sycamores flowering
    In a land torn by strife and unrest.
Sunny days when the turf heaps we mounded.
    While the blackbird sang loud in the boughs
Cold and cloying the mud where we floundered
    Through the bog in pursuit of the cows.
Sweet the glasses of stout we upended
    In the bar at the close of the day
Races gay at the Curragh attended
    Brought me happiness, Kitty O'Shea.

Vagrant son for his old comrades yearning
    Homeward bound for the place of his birth
To the roads of the outback returning
    In a country the greatest on earth.
Where the old bush delivers her bounty
    Under skies always cloudless and blue
Far removed from green meadow and county
    And a dream that has failed to come true.
Still melodious lingers your laughter
    And unyielding my spirit will pray
That we meet in the doubtful hereafter
    Fond farewell to you, Kitty O'Shea.

Dublin

Sombre buildings sit sternly abysmal
   Unattractive as tombs of the dead
Slanting rain sprinkles baptism dismal
   On the statues of martyrs who bled.
Deep the Liffey, dark artery repulsive
   Shifting slow between walls stained and stark
Flow of traffic detained and convulsive
   Over bitumen shiny and dark.

Where the crowds rush advancing, receding
   Like the fall and the rise of a tide
And the vultures society unheeding
   Their time in the alleyways bide.
Spacious churches and saints made of plaster
   Where defeated the true gods must flee
Leaving Mammon remaining the master
   In the bloody decades yet to be.

Little hope for the future apparent
   In a land by the war-god beguiled
From the North spreads the violence inherent
   Like the plagues that in Egypt defiled.
No gay beauty of Nature attending
   To relieve the dull work of mankind
With your record infamous ascending
   Strumpet city, I leave you behind.

An Irish Prayer
(St Patrick's Day, 1983)

Cold emerald meadows silent, undulating
    Brooding under troubled skies
Bare sycamores like sentenced martyrs waiting
    Where the peat-bog lies.

Cloying mists, like Ireland's sombre sorrow
    Slowly drifting sad and pale
The clouds must lift, the sun may shine tomorrow
    Will our faith prevail?

Help us Lord to find an understanding
    With the stubborn English and their laws
Help us to stand firm and strong, demanding
    Justice for our cause.

An Irish Prophecy

On the top of a toadstool a leprechaun sat
   By a bog on the road to Killarney
He smoked a clay pipe, wore a little green hat
   And he lived 'neath the castle of Blarney.
A goblin came by, he was friendly and stout
   And he said with sad smile on his features
"The English from Belfast have driven me out
   There will soon be no room for poor creatures."

Said the leprechaun "Fear not, the day will arrive
   When the tyrants will suffer eviction
For brave martyrs like Wolf Tone in vain did not strive
   We will conquer hard rule and restriction.
"Like our patriots brave, stand determined and dour
   Put true faith in each Fenian brother
For the great powers-that-be in their hunger for power
   In the end will destroy one another.

For the Irish were always a stout-hearted band
   Long resisting oppressive damnation
The true Paddies will govern our beautiful land
   When old England's no longer a nation."

Homesick
(Ireland 1983)

The peat fire flickers its friendly flame
   Filled with a blue and luminous light
Cosy and warm, but it isn't the same
   As the coolibah coals in the Austral night.
Sweet sings the thrush in the Kerry dawn
   But sooner the scribe would like to hear
The kookaburras' chorus at early morn
   On the big dry plains that are burned and bare.

Picturesque lie the Killarney lakes
   Peaceful and still 'neath a wintry sun
But I long for the glitter the saltbush makes
   On the far spread miles of a Western run.
Silent and mellow the Irish night
   Spreading its shawl under cold white stars
But give me the bush when the moon is bright
   And dawn winds rustle the black belars.

In sycamore boughs 'mid blossoms sweet
   The mavis renders a musical score
But I dream of somnolent, drowsy heat
   On a wilga ridge where the bush crows caw.
Homesick of late your poet grows
   For the wild wide acres that gave him birth
He must soon go back where the drought wind blows
   In the greatest country on all the earth.

To An Irish Girl

It's lonesome in the Cross tonight
  My flat is cold and drear
The little pub is close nearby
  Where once you pulled the beer
When stranger than all fear and doubt
  My faith in you prevailed
In happy days a world away
  Before you homeward sailed.

Again I see you as you serve
  The liquor of our choice
Grey eyes beneath the dark red curls
  The soft Killarney voice.
When first I met you in the bar
  By love I was obsessed
I loved you greater when to me
  Your sin you had confessed.

The bitter secret that you told
  That caused your heart to break
Of how your happiness was sold
  For dull religion's sake
Though younger far you were in years
  And better traits could claim
Our wild rebellious Irish ways
  Were very much the same.

And though I took things pretty hard
  The day we had to part
'Twas you restored the will to fight
  Back to my troubled heart
Though human weakness took its toll
  And brutal creed defamed
My deepest love belongs to you
  The girl the Convent claimed.

The Singer in the Bar

He was voluble and friendly
　　As the Paddies mostly are
The man whose singing drew a crowd
　　That day in Canty's bar.
I gained no introduction
　　And I never learned his name
But his glorious drunken melody
　　I remember just the same.

Quite a lot of tipsy workmen
　　Were gathered round to hear
The lilting of his tuneful voice
　　Well oiled by stout and beer.
And from many bleary eyes I saw
　　Reluctant tear-drops start
As his love for troubled Ireland
　　He delivered from the heart.

The old and hallowed Irish songs
　　Rolled richly off his tongue
Great classics that I hadn't heard
　　Since days when I was young.
Rendered by an unknown labourer.
　　At a back street bar in Cork
Songs immortal long forgotten
　　As the pop stars yowl and squawk.

Sad refrains of fearless martyrs
　　Who had died to free the Green
Talent you would never witness
　　On a television screen.
'Till the final notes ascended
　　To a stirring climax loud

And entranced with deep emotion
  Was the eagerly listening crowd.

Then a pair of burly garda
  Came and told him to desist
So I walked away disgusted
  In the shrouding rain and mist.
And I since have often pondered
  On a fact grown very plain
Many men of obvious talent
  Cannot sell their skills for gain.

Never finding loftier status
  Than the use of laymens' tools
Dying on a pick and shovel
  Rich society's willing fools.
While we reap dull entertainment
  On the radio and TV
From uninteresting performers
  Who command a massive fee.

And the talent scouts unworldly
  Who do little else than talk
Should frequent unlikely places
  Like the back-street bars in Cork.

Salute the Brave
(A rhyme about heroism)

A Digger sat with a deal of foreboding
  Watching the German shells exploding,
While all around his mates were reloading.
  He said "I see no medals gleaming,
  But lots of deadly shrapnel screaming
And blood from wounded soldiers streaming."

"When nightfall makes a dark diversion
  I'll take a very quick excursion;
I hold no qualms about desertion."

He hid beneath a heap of rubble
  And after dark, with little trouble,
He made for Switzerland at the double.

And there he met a stunning sheila
  Whose father was a diamond dealer;
It didn't take him long to wheel her.

She soon responded to his notions
  And bought him alcoholic potions
And rubbed him down with sunburn lotions.

She married him and kept on spending
  Her daddy's pile of cash unending,
To all her husband's needs attending.

Her love and money comfort brought him
  And for a while the Army sought him,
But brutal provosts never caught him.

His Digger mates, and they were many,

Were all discharged without a penny
To find a job; there wasn't any.

So readers, always think before
    You go away to fight a war.
Dream not of bayonets smeared with gore.

Or decorations, beer and dinners
    For shot and mutilated sinners
The brave men seldom end up winners.

The Enlightened New-Chum

The sea of life goes rolling on
    but slowly ebbs the tides
Old scenes return, and vagrant thought
    oft with the past abides.
And though my memory I admit
    is well on the decline
I still recall when Duncan cooked
    a placid porcupine.

A substitute for mutton chops
    or when beef is hard to find
This prickly little native son
    for good eating is designed.
Well scalded to remove the spines
    and carefully packed in clay
With breadcrumbs stuffed, his carcase fat
    in smouldering ashes lay.

And just as we had settled down
    to eat a grisly feed
A callow new-chum came along
    astride a prancing steed.
An unenlightened bloke it seemed
    with pale and vacant dial
His English coat was neatly cut,
    his jodphurs latest style.

A simple greenhorn, so we thought
    from England's shores afar
Said Duncan "Have some dinner, mate
    it's Barwon Caviar.
"A bonzer feed we just dished up
    from fresh corroboree legs

The liver of a wampus
and a dozen bunyip eggs."

The new-chum took a knife and fork
"Bai Jove, it looks a treat"
He cut a slice of porcupine
and settled down to eat.
He showed his vacant smile and said
"Bai Jove, this meal is grand
But we present a better dish
Back in my native land.

"A nice fat weasel a la carte
served up with batsblood sauce
A dressing made of badger's brains
and leaves and roots of gorse.
We also have a hedgehog pie
from a little chap with spines
Bai Jove, y'know he looks just like
your local porcupines."

And with his vacant smile affixed
he calmly rode away
While Duncan and myself stood still
with not a word to say.
And when I tell you this old mate
don't rouse or make a fuss
Not always are the new-chums green
it's often blokes like us.

Beefwood Hotel

My father kept the Beefwood pub
   in days long gone before
There were no modern comforts then
   the land was hard and raw.
Across the wide Tuloona plains
   he saw the teamsters come
With black tobacco in their pipes
   and pints to fill with rum.
The squatters came to hold a spree
   when Christmas tide would fall
Some shouted gladly for the bar
   some shouted not at all.
Wild bearded drovers from the North
   brought tales from farther out
Of hard times spent on Queensland runs
   besieged by flood and drought.

The down-and-outs in search of work
   would drop their slender swags
In hopes the pub could spare some grub
   to fill their tucker bags
And shearers when a shed cut out
   with joy the bar would breast.
Remorseful when the cheques were gone
   they headed farther west.

But now the scene for aye has changed
   the old bush pub is gone
And where it stood in bygone times
   the tractors thunder on.
No more are wild carousals held
   that end in song and fight
And silent is the lonely plain
   where curlews called at night.

The cotton kings from overseas
    plough deep the blacksoil loam
But when the moon sheds ghostly light
    perhaps the spectres roam
Of hardened men who won the land,
    by time now swept away
But still with them on history's page
    the old pub lives today.

Song of the Vagabond Shearers

We've shorn the sheep and drawn our cheques
    We're happy to cut out
The time has come to wet our necks
    With whiskey, beer and stout.
And when our cash is down the drain
    And aching hard each head
We hit the blacksoil road again
    To seek another shed.

CHORUS...
Let's hit the blacksoil road again
    And travel fast and far
The winter days are on the wane
    There's beer in every bar.
There's cod to catch along the Bree
    So rise and hump your load
We're not financial but we're free
    Let's hit the blacksoil road.

The squatter men are not too bad
    We cadge some flour and meat
There's lots of bunnies to be had
    When roasted, quite a treat.
There's sheep unshorn across the plain
    From Walgett clear to Bourke
So take the blacksoil road again
    And try to find some work.

CHORUS...
Let's hit the blacksoil road again
    There's naught to daunt or fear
So look alive and we'll survive
    While there's a sheep to shear.
We toil and spend, we lose and gain

We take and also give
So hit the blacksoil road again
And find a way to live.

And when we cut the wool once more
To seek a pub we go
Just like we always did before
Our weighty cheques to blow.
No goal or glory we attain
And when we're stony broke
We take the blacksoil road again
To shoulder fortune's yoke.

CHORUS...
So hit the blacksoil road again
Without the least delay
Let's share the sorrow, joy and pain
That comes from day to day.
By ridge and river, hill and plain
There's room for you and me
Let's hit the blacksoil road again
For vagabonds are free.

Wild Cats

("The bush is full of feral cats. I don't know where they all come from" —
Paddy Austin, professional hunter.)

Our forebears prowled when Egypt's might was great
    Rebels we were for long decades B.C.
Never conforming, learning all laws to hate
    'Ere Peter fished in the blue depths of Gallilee.
We leave the allotted placed beside the stove
    The generous saucer of warm milk we spurn.
Through the wild fastness of the bush we rove
    Scorning man's gentle bondage, never to return.

The shy and follish rabbit is our prey
    The helpless fledglings from the nest are torn.
Disposers swift we are of fowls that stray
    We raid the hen-coop in the dewy light of dawn.
Gripped by hot lust we roam in moonshine bright
    Savage and swift our loves we consumate
Blood-curdling yowls make hideous the night
    As in the cactus clumps we copulate.

In the dark scrubs we rear our banal brood
    Charged with deep instinct for survival hard
Relentless searchers in incessant search for food
    Showing all laws contemptuous disregard.
Wild outcasts of domesticity, pawns of fate
    Banished to lonely den in hollow tree
Doomed by swift bullet, trap or poison bait
    The rebellious life we live is short but free.

The Old Desire

Springtime has come and the bush is green
   And the big buck kangaroo seeks his doe
While romantic wombats their whiskers preen
Where the wombat-esses with love-light glow.
The possums chatter in the gum trees' tops
   And pursue their paramours with prideful lust
And the elegant emu endearing flops
   Beside his hen in a pool of dust.
The amorous Arunta sharpens his spears
   And looks for a quee-ai dark and entrancing
In Arnhem Land where the buffalo stares
   At a plumb young cow with a heart romancing.

The dashing dingo records refrains
   To his sly red mate when the moon is mellow
While the brolga dances on dank bore-drains
   And his concubines think he's a handsome fellow.
The bandy-bandy displays his rings
   Of black and white to this girl-friend proudly
The meticulous magpie a serenade sings
   And his hen bird warbles a love song loudly.
The drover discloses his wants and cares
   To the servant girl on an outback station
And the drunken shearer lecherous leers
   At the barmaid who plans his degradation.

The platypus plies his romantic tastes
   On his duck-billed cliner in waters shallow
And exceptional effort the blue-tongue wastes
   To win a lover both hard and callow.
The frilly lizard lingering lurks
   By a strainer post where his love sits sunning
The piratical pelican prances and perks
   To entrance a mate where slow streams are running.

The carpet snake casts a conniving coil
    Around his sinister sweetheart scaley
The erotic echidna scratches the soil
    While the spike-sprinkled sheila chatters gaily.

All the world's creatures love in the spring
    With the ceaseless desire and longing lusty
And will still be doing the very same thing
    Long after your poet's bones are musty.

Coober Pedy

I'll sing a song about a town
Dumped on a desert baked and brown
    Drear and drack location
Whirly-winds go round and round
Men dig homes beneath the ground
Poisonous reptiles fierce abound
    Causing consternation.
Through the arid fastness wide
Trickles slow a human tide
    Man for wealth is greedy
Seeking hard the opal's beam
Hoping fortune's grin will gleam
Frantic search for fleeting dream
    Out at Coober Pedy.

Men with little coin to lose
Pawns of fate, addicts to booze
    Scorning regulations
Adventurers from Argentine
The Asian and the European
The short and fat, the long and lean
    Flotsam of all nations.
Roving men of every race
Social lions who fell from grace
    Transients poor and needy
Honest coves you trust on sight
Worthless bludgers on the bite
Tucker short and finance tight
    Out at Coober Pedy.

Spawning ground of crime and theft
Lives of love and joy bereft
    Small the chance of winning

Status great or fortune grand.
Hopeful wish and empty hand
Lonely graves in shifting sand
    Wages for the sinning.
Still the dream remains alive
In their dotage still they strive
    Decadent and seedy
Pile of potch a holy plot
Where the bold ambitions rot
Disillusioned, caring not
    Out at Coober Pedy.

Old Explorers

The old explorers British bred
  Across Australia lined out
In saffron dawns and sunsets red
They didn't know what lay ahead
  But still they had to find out.

Through mountain torrents foaming white
  By craggy peaks unscalable
On desert fastness burning bright
They struggled forward day and night
  With courage unassailable.

Strong fortitude that sought to flout
  Old Nature's mighty forces
Determination thwarting doubt
And when the grub supply ran out
  They killed and ate their horses.

Cruel summer heat that boiled the blood
  And snows that winter flaunted
The barriers of drought and flood
The blacksoil plains that turned to mud
  They faced them all undaunted.

Did they the Saviour's mercy seek
  When hours of life seemed numbered
When dry were waterhole and creek
When spirit sagged and flesh was weak
  And Death watched while they slumbered?

A durable and reckless band
  Heroes of great tradition
They fought and died to win a land

That foreigners today demand
    With covetous ambition.

Their creed was "forward and attack"
    The fate of some is mystery
Unhallowed grave by unmarked track.
To fame and fortune some came back
    They still live on in history.

The Perfect Woman

(Garv's honest opinion, with apologies
to supporters of Womens Lib)

The little creatures in the bush
   To tell the honest truth
Remind me of the females frail
   That I knew in my youth.
One time a lady friend I had
   Brunette, petite and small
And she was like a wombat
   She couldn't see at all.
She couldn't see my happiness
   In drinking various grogs
Or betting on the horses
   And the pools and coursing dogs.

The next was like a magpie
   She would flit from spot to spot
She screamed and scolded madly
   But she didn't say a lot.
A senseless bird whose ranting voice
   My temper quickly soured
And ceaselessly she bashed my lugs
   'Til they were cauliflowered.

So I found another Sheila
   This time like a native bear
She wasted lots of greenstuff
   And she didn't have a care
About the way she blew my cash
   On dresses smart and shoes
And wouldn't heed me when I said
   I wanted it for booze.

But now I have discovered

A girl of sterling worth
She's like the small marsupial moles
That live north-west of Perth.
She's interested not at all
In gaudy garments glad
She doesn't eat much tucker
And she stays inside the pad.
A girl to suit me better
I could never ever find
For like the small marsupial moles
She's deaf and dumb and blind.

Gums Beside the River

(Told to the author in his youth by an old Swagman).

I've travelled many outback ways
   When heat was like a hell-fire
And tramped in storms when lightning' plays
   And thunder rolls like shell-fire.
Slunk like a felon late at night
   Through private land unbidden
And peaceful slept when stars were bright
   By rubbish-tip and midden.
But when a bloke is real beat out
   And his legs begin to quiver
There ain't a better spot, no doubt
   Than gums beside a river.

Some bitter summer walks I've had
   On black-soil deserts gleamin'
When the heat-haze dances wild and mad
   Just like a fiery demon.
No water in the bloody bag
   And yer give up hope of winnin'
When yer weary feet begin to lag
   And the carrion crows are grinnin'.
No moisture cool, the grass all dead
   Faint hope begins to wither
Then yer jump with joy as yer see ahead
   The gums beside the river.

I've seen the mighty Harbour Bridge
   That tourists all are praisin'
The shinin' gems at Lightnin' Ridge
   And other sights amazin'
The poundin' waves on coastal shores
   The verdant Riverina

The steamin' hot artesian bores
  Nor'-west where times are leaner.
But the camp I always reckon best
  Is where weepin' willows shiver
And yer drop yer swag and peaceful rest
  Under gums beside the river.

And when I make the final plod
  To Heaven's golden gateway
I'm pretty confident that God
  Will send me up the straightway
To where the skies are always bright
  With silver glories painted
And there ain't no flies or sandy blight
  And the tucker don't get tainted
I'll hear St Peter softly say
  "Old camper, come thou hither"
And with golden staff he'll point the way
  To the gums beside the river.

Dinner with Duncan

When Duncan cooks a roast of meat
  So succulent and brown
You take my oath, it's quite a treat
  And beats the meals in town.
The old camp-oven sizzles loud
  And Boozer chews a bone
While Duncan on an oil-drum sits
  And smokes a roll-yer-own.

Under the wilgas green and cool
  Where magpies squawk and play
And overbearing bureaucrats
  Are far enough away
To make a freedom rough complete
  Where silence reigns supreme
No garish lamps throw sickly light
  No motors honk and scream.

A scene that to the past belongs
  When bushmen all were free
And made a camp in peace and quiet
  Beneath a shady tree.
Then in the river threw a line
  In hopes the fish would bite
And told tall tales and sang old songs
  When gleamed the moon's pale light.

And though with poverty and want
  They oft walked hand in hand
They had no regulations small
  That now engulf the land.
Though scarce the work, with comforts few
  And small and mean the pay

289

They gave the future little thought
  And lived from day to day.

So now in efforts to escape
  The modern rat-race grim
I journey down to Duncan's camp
  To share a meal with him
In bush serene; a tasty dish
  No restaurant could boast
When Duncan hangs the oven up
  And cooks a juicy roast.

The Failures

You meet them battling for a quid in every walk of life
    Some born in wealth, and some of families poor
Tired victims of adversity, the spawn of woe and strife
    The blokes who had to go and failed to score.
They were here at the beginning, before Egypt, Greece and
Crete
    In the days of Carthage, and the might of ancient Rome
Born to live in sad misfortune, losers owning loss complete
    Luckless triers without comfort, hope or home.

When the ruthless English tyrants flogged and starved the
lesser men
    And the Yankees bought and sold the Negro slaves
And the brutal Arab traders showed no shame or pity when
    They lined the eastern roads with nameless graves
They were plentiful as rabbits in the drear depression years
    Drovers, labourers and the hated men who "shore"
Agents, speculators, dealers by the system brought to tears
    The blokes who had a go, and failed to score.

Floating, shaky, shabby projects sometimes not within the
law
    Pinning false hopes on a shifty shady deal
Taking on some doubtful business where the rule is fang
and claw
    Tricks of confidence that hide a bare-faced steal.
There are those who nearly made it and succumbed too oft
to booze
    Others by a faithless woman were betrayed
Gamblers bold who followed horses that they reckoned
couldn't lose
    And the ones by fickle Lady Luck gainsayed.

By the hands of time defeated, to a hostel gone at last
    Or to humpies in the far remote bush towns
Sinking into insignificance, deteriorating fast

A group of disillusioned beaten clowns.
But perhaps when old St Peter first and final judgement
makes
And they cross the Jordan to a kinder shore
In the glorious hereafter, then perhaps they'll get the breaks
The blokes who had a go and failed to score.

Damper and Tea

When a drought seems never-ending and the price of wool
is falling
    And a PLEASE EXPLAIN is noted on the foot of every
bill
And the bank for a reduction of your overdraft is calling
    It is then you sit and wonder how you live and if you will.
When the tanks are nearly empty and the river ceases
flowing
    Or when floods are on the country and the plains are like a
sea
Though your hopes are fast declining it's a simple pleasure
knowing
There's a damper in the oven and a billy full of tea.
        It's a simple pleasure knowing ,
        When the winds of fate are blowing
        That there's damper in the oven and a billy full of tea.

Oft we dream of costly dinners in a restaurant cool and
pleasant
    Where society ladies gather in their jewels and evening
dress
While the waiters starched and stately serve expensive wine
and pheasant
    Far from outback occupations with their endless strain
and stress.
But on Western tracks in winter when the icy rain is
swishing
And your motor's bogged and boiling on the road from
Bourke to Bree
Though your far-off home be humble, for that home you're
sadly wishing
    With a damper in the oven and a billy full of tea.
        For that home you're sadly wishin'

It's a better proposition
With the oven full of damper and a billy full of tea.

Heed ye well my simple verses, thoughtless sinner
unenlightened
  When the hand of fickle fortune seems to show you small
regard
It is then by lesser comforts that our lives are mostly
brightened
  And the future looks more hopeful and the road ahead
less hard.
Call on fortitude and courage, cast aside all care and sorrow
  Always chances for a battler in this country wide and free
For it cannot rain forever and the sun will shine tomorrow
  Still there's damper in the oven and a billy full of tea.
    Yes the sun will shine tomorrow
    There's a meal to lend or borrow
    While the damper's in the oven
    and the billy's full of tea.

The Nightjar

The nightjar, as I will explain
   Is not made out of porcelain
Nor does it sit, with nasty smell
   'Neath beds in unsewered hotel.
It isn't emptied with great care
   By chambermaids of yesteryear
Then washed and polished clean and bright
   In preparation for the night.
It's just a predatory fowl
   A species of Australian owl.

A loafer, bushmen will attest
   That doesn't even build a nest
But lays it's egg in forests dark
   Upon the ground 'mid leaves and bark.
And right from dusk to morning light
   It's jarring cackle jars the night
As for nocturnal prey it searches
   Or in the clumps of timber perches.
And then full fed it sleeps all day
   In feathers white and brown and grey.

From Yarra River to Wannarring
   You'll hear the nightjars' ceaseless jarring
Like modern ockers drunk and hearty
   And ladies at a social party.
And of the three, I must confess
   The nightjar jars me somewhat less.
A cunning bird of small misdeed
   It's depredations don't impede
Mankind, whose greed destroys and smothers.
   A greater criminal than all others.

The Native Wattle

The native wattle, poets tell
  Delights you with its fragrant smell
An emblem bright, our national flower
  The tourists praise it by the hour
Entrancing are its gay perfumes
  When in the August days it blooms
So claim most bards, but this one thinks
  The native wattle really stinks
Just camp beside it in a breeze
  It's awful smell will make you sneeze
A sickening odour, strong and cloying
  That human noses find annoying
And I would dearly love to throttle
  The bards who rave about the wattle.

When at its worst its quite a lever
  To cause and aggravate hay fever
And when the blossoms fall and break up
  It's like a sheila without make-up
Twisted and hard, it seems to me
  To lack all graceful symmetry
Its golden gleam scarce lasts a day
  And then it's ugly plain and grey
The golden flowers are quick to fade
  Like tawdry friendships that are made
The solid blooms that stand the strain
  Are mostly pretty poor and plain.
The bush bards who revere the wattle
  Would drive a strong man to the bottle.

Follow the Darling

Tourist and traveller this land is wide
  The cities are dull and staid
Free and unspoiled is the far outback
  Travel it unafraid.
Land where freedom is vanishing fast
  Though ghosts of it still remain
Follow the Darling out to Bourke
  Over the blacksoil plain.

Watch the inquisitive emu roam
  Angle where big cods bite
Listen with rapture to old bush tales
  Told round the fire at night.
Where once the camels went lurching by
  And the steamboats forward pressed —
Follow the Darling down to Bourke
  Follow the old tracks west.

The parakeets flit like flames of fire
  The pelicans paddle slow
And the indigo blooms of the desert pea
  Like sunburnished beacons glow.
Unlimited acres of Mitchell grass
  In seasons of storm and rain —
Follow the Darling out to Bourke
  Over the blacksoil plain.

Yarran and wilga on sandhills dun
  Mulga that glistens grey
And no cloud eclipses the summer sun
  From dawn til the end of day.
Shearers on strike and squatters incensed
  In years when the fleece was gold —

Follow the Darling out to Bourke
   For historical wealth untold.

Where Lawson and Ogilvie wrote the songs
   Of a lavish unconquered land
And bullock and horse teams drew the wool
   Where cotton now holds command.
Shearers and squatters and droving men
   A few of them still remain
So follow the Darling out to Bourke
   Live with the past again.
   Live with the past again.

Dental Disorder

(A tribute to Bernie, a practical practitioner and
Peggy, his receptionist)

Wisdom tooth is aching
   fit to make you reel
Time to see the dentist
   Bernard H O'Neill.
Go into the surgery
   shaking bad with fright
Place looks like a morgue house
   awful cold and white.

Peggy with a happy smile
   will very soon appear
Wouldn't look so confident
   if she was in the chair.
Bernie gets the needle out
   drives it in your gum
While you long for brandy
   whisky beer or rum.

Soon there is no feeling
   in your mouth at all
Bernie with professional skill
   prods it with his awl.
Peggy still is full of smiles
   thinks it's all a lark
Now the forceps fasten on
   like a hungry shark.

Bernie rocks the pressure in
   feel him strain and lift
Rooted in the jawbone deep
   the old fang's hard to shift.

A mighty heave and out it comes
    wasn't any pain
Just the same you wouldn't want
    to have it done again.

Spit the blood into a bowl
    lean against the wall
Then pull out your cheque book
    for the hardest part of all.